Wolves in Ireland

WOLVES IN IRELAND

a natural and cultural history

Kieran Hickey

OPEN AIR

Typeset in 11pt on 13pt Ehrhardt
by Carrigboy Typesetting Services for
OPEN AIR an imprint of FOUR COURTS PRESS LTD
7 Malpas Street, Dublin 8, Ireland
www.fourcourtspress.ie
and in North America for
FOUR COURTS PRESS
c/o ISBS, 920 N.E. 58th Avenue, Suite 300, Portland, OR 97213.

First published 2011.
Paperback edition 2013.

A catalogue record for this title is available
from the British Library.

ISBN 978-1-84682-423-4

This publication was grant-aided by the Heritage Council under the
Heritage Education, Community and Outreach Scheme 2011.

Printed in Ireland
by SPRINT-Print, Dublin

This book is dedicated to the memory of three lost friends

Sean Condon

Norman Price

Ignacio Lozano–Gonzales

Contents

Figures, tables and plates

FIGURES

TABLES

COLOUR PLATES
(between page 64 and page 65)

Acknowledgments

Firstly, my thanks to the Heritage Council for their generous financial support for this project. Secondly, my thanks must go to a vast array of people, too numerous to mention by name, for huge help and assistance. This was especially significant given the broad nature of this work and the effort over almost the last two decades. In no particular order, these people include Tim Collins, Kieran Hoare and others in the James Hardiman Library, National University of Ireland (NUI), Galway, Conor Newman, Department of Archaeology, NUI Galway, Laura Finnegan, George Reynolds and many other individual correspondents.

A special thanks to those who contributed significant help and expertise to the names chapter, in particular the Irish language component. I am grateful to Nollaig Ó Muraíle and Aengus Finnegan, Roinn na Gaeilge, NUI Galway, Conchubhar Ó Crualaoich, An Brainse Logainmneacha, An Roinn Gnóthaí Pobail, and Pól Mac Cana.

My thanks to three anonymous reviewers who helped shape the text. A very important and special thanks to Michael Potterton who had the unenviable task of editing my ramblings into a coherent text and to Anthony Tierney and all at Four Courts Press for their support. Thanks also to Dr Siúbhan Comer, Department of Geography, NUI Galway, for figure 2.1. I am very grateful to Gary Wilson for allowing me to use some of his excellent photographs of wolves in Dublin Zoo.

Support from my friends, colleagues in the School of Geography and Archaeology and elsewhere throughout the university and, most importantly, my family, was crucial in completing this project. These people will be greatly relieved that I have finally finished the book and they won't have to listen to me going on about this any longer; well, for a while at least.

All errors and omissions are my own fault of course, but hopefully these are not too many. To you, the reader, I welcome any additional information of any sort on wolves in Ireland that you can send me, no matter how trivial.

Galway, July 2011

CHAPTER I

Introduction

WHY A BOOK ON WOLVES IN IRELAND?

The howling of wolves has been described by some as one of the most terrifying sounds in nature and by others as one of the most exhilarating (pls 3, 7). To our ancestors in Ireland, it must have been a sound that many were familiar with. It is hard to imagine in modern Ireland, with its well manicured farmland and heavily modified forests and bogs, the wildness of many parts of the country only a few centuries ago. It was a wilderness in which wolves moved in small packs, hunted and bred beside human settlements and often enough came into contact with them. To a pack of hungry wolves, or even a lone wolf, an unguarded flock of sheep in a field or enclosure was as easy a meal as they were ever likely to get. Yet the Irish wolf was far more than just a dark and dangerous predator out in the mountains and forest or just another part of our natural history. The wolf has permeated so many aspects of our cultural history as well, along with our ever-evolving relationship with the landscape and our changing attitudes towards nature. Wolves still permeate our language, although most people never stop to think where such common expressions as 'keep the wolf from the door', 'hungry as a wolf', 'wolf it down', 'cry wolf' and 'wolf whistle' have come from.

This book explores both the natural and the cultural history of wolves in Ireland, tapping into the vast array of historical and other documentary data on the subject. Firstly, it examines the archaeological evidence on wolves in Ireland stretching from the last Ice Age up to medieval times (wolves of course being around Ireland far longer than humans). Next, the place-names and other name information are examined, showing how a range of wolf references have been hidden away in the several names for 'wolf' in Irish. There is also an amazing variety of folklore associated with the Irish wolf, and this too is examined.

This is followed by a detailed outline and analysis of the records of wolf encounters and incidents right up to 1786 and possibly beyond. Of course the existence of the Irish wolf-dog or Irish wolfhound shows just how much wolves were a part of the Irish landscape and reflects their interactions with humans. One of the key questions this research addresses is whether wolves were rare or common and this is discussed along with the ways in which the wolf survived in Ireland. The penultimate chapter discusses the causes of the decline and extermination of the Irish wolf and how a whole series of circumstances effectively eliminated them from the landscape. The final chapter identifies key issues relating to the Irish wolf going forward, including the question of reintroduction.

This book would not have been possible without the previous work on wolves in Ireland by two individuals: J.E. Harting's seminal work on extinct animals in Britain, published in 1880, and James Fairley's many academic and bibliographic works or Irish mammals.[1]

LAST WOLVES IN IRELAND AND BRITAIN

Ireland has only about fourteen native species of mammal and four of these (the wild boar, wild cat, brown bear and wolf (fig. 1.1)) are no longer present.[2] In recent times, however, some wild boars have escaped from a number of specialized farms around the country and there is the possibility that a new wild breeding population may establish itself in the future. Whereas the first three have been gone from Ireland for at least a thousand years, the wolf was probably present right up to AD1786 and possibly as late as the early 1800s. This is in contrast to England, Scotland and Wales, where wolves had been exterminated much earlier.

It is likely that the last wolves in England were wiped out in the early part of the fourteenth century. It was certainly not before that, as eight cattle were recorded as being killed by wolves at Rossendale in Lancashire in 1304–5.[3] It is not clear when the last wolf was killed in Wales, but is likely to have been around the same time. There is no doubt that they survived much later in Scotland – at least as late as 1684 and possibly later. Lecky reported that the last wolf in Scotland was killed around 1680 by Sir Ewan Cameron.[4] According to other traditions, the last wolf in Britain was killed in Sutherland in Scotland in 1743.[5] This later date for Scotland is heavily disputed by Yalden, however, and the dates given by Buczacki for England are much more realistic.[6]

Remarkably, despite their incredibly bad press throughout the millennia, wolf numbers are on the increase across Western Europe and the USA. This has occurred as a result of heavy protection in many countries, and wolves are also naturally reintroducing themselves to areas where they had previously been exterminated. A recent example of this is Switzerland, which has wolves again for the first time since the early part of the twentieth century.[7] They have also become a significant issue in the Alpes

1.1 A grey wolf in Dublin Zoo, 2011 (photograph courtesy of Gary Wilson).

Maritimes area of eastern France, and wolves are spreading from the mountains into the lowlands and even to the edges of cities, much like in medieval times.[8] In the USA, where all wolves had been exterminated in virtually the entire lower forty-eight states, they have made a dramatic return over the last fifteen years, under heavy protection. Old conflicts between some farmers and hunters and wolves have now been reopened.[9]

As plate 2 shows, however, the current range of the grey wolf (*Canis lupus*) is far narrower than it used to be and the recoveries so far have been associated with very small numbers of wolves. In North America, their loss in both Mexico and the USA is obvious. On the Eurasian continent, their loss is most evident throughout most of Western Europe, the Middle East, India, China and Japan, while they have also been lost throughout North Africa and parts of the Arabian Peninsula. They still thrive in Alaska, Canada, Russia and some of the former USSR states, however, as well as in parts of northern Asia including Mongolia.

WOLF–HUMAN INTERACTIONS

The relationship between wolves and humans goes back a long time. Wolves were probably the first wild animals to be used by humans. It may well have started as a mutually beneficial partnership, as humans and wolves both sought the same prey. Wolves could track much more effectively than humans as a result of their sensitive noses. Humans, with primitive weapons such as spears, could wound and cripple an animal without getting too close. So it is possible that both species hunted together and shared the spoils. The relationship was made easier by the fact that wolves are by nature social animals, accustomed to accept leadership from a dominant individual. In this way, the human hunter acquired a pack of canine helpers.[10] This still occurs today, where dogs are used to hunt prey with humans in the forests of Papua New Guinea. The modern practice of hunting with dogs can most likely be traced back to these early partnerships between humans and wolves.

In addition, modern genetic studies have shown that all domestic dogs (*Canis familiaris*) are originally descended from the grey wolf (*Canis lupus*), which was first domesticated in Asia around 15,000 years ago.[11]

SOME BASIC WOLF FACTS

The wolf is from the order *Carnivora* ('meat-eaters'), family *Canidae* (dog family). The wolf species that this book is concerned with is *Canis lupus*, which has the more common names of grey wolf, Arctic wolf or timber wolf. Other wolf species include the maned wolf (*Chrysocyon brachyurus*), which occurs in South America,[12] and the Ethiopian wolf (*Canis simensis*), which only lives in Ethiopia.[13] There are fewer than 500 Ethiopian wolves alive today and they are seriously endangered, especially as a result of rabies. More remarkably, in 2011, DNA results showed that an animal known as the Egyptian jackal (*Canis aureus lupaster*), is not a jackal at all, and is in fact directly related to the grey wolf and should be renamed as the African wolf.[14] This discovery was made in Ethiopia, meaning that that country has two very distinct wolf species. The red wolf (*Canis rufus*) is very rare and hardly exists in the wild, occurring only in south-eastern USA and Mexico.[15] In fact, it is disputed whether it is a true species or in fact a sub-species of the grey wolf.

There is at least one known species of wolf that has become extinct in the last 13,000 years or so. The dire wolf (*Canis dirus*) was enormous by modern wolf standards and its loss is part of the loss of megafauna throughout the world since the end of the last Ice Age, partly as a result of human activities but also rapid climate change. Its bones have only been found on the North American continent. At the sub-species level, a number of classifications exist which show that there are possibly

1.2 The last Tasmanian wolf in captivity (Hobart Zoo, 1933). Some survived in the wild into the 1940s, but they are now extinct.

numerous wolf sub-species with distinctive characteristics. An example is the Mexican wolf (*Canis lupus baileyi*), which is only found in Mexico and southern USA.[16]

To add to the complexity, numerous species of all sorts have been given the tag 'wolf', from insects to fish to other large animals (see table 1.1 for a list of some of these). One most obvious example and sadly another large species that became extinct in 1936 is the Thylacine (*Thylacinus cyanocephalus*), also known as the Tasmanian wolf, so-called because the last surviving population was only found in Tasmania (fig. 1.2).[17] However, the Tasmanian wolf is not directly related to the grey wolf or any other wolf species as it was a marsupial predator. The tag 'wolf' was used to imply a ferocious creature.

The geographical range of the grey wolf is enormous and it was at one time the most common mammal after humans and farm animals. The nearest populations to Ireland are in Eastern Europe (although there are some isolated populations in Spain and Italy), east to India, Russia, Canada and the USA. The wolf was the most widely distributed mammal globally after humans, before rats, mice and other species were carried around the world by humans. The current estimated world population is in excess of 120,000, of which 50,000 occur in the Asian region of Russia.[18] Of this figure, fewer than one thousand survive in northern Europe, with a few isolated populations in southern Europe.[19] The preferred habitat of

Table 1.1 List of species with 'wolf' in their name.

| Fauna | | | |
English	Latin	Meaning	Source
Tasmanian wolf/ Thylacine	*Thylacinus cyanocephalus*		Flannery & Schouten (2001)
Faklands Island dog/ wolf	*Dusicyon australis*		Flannery & Schouten (2001)
Aardwolf	*Proteles cristata*	earth-wolf	Koehler & Richardson (1990)
Wolverine	*Gulo gulo*	glutton	Attenborough (2002)
Northern pike	*Esox lucius*	water-wolf	Thomas (2004)
Wolf-fish or Ocean catfish	*Anarhichas lupus*		Brookes (1743)
Sea-wolf or wolf-fish	*Lupus marinus*		Brookes (1743)
Wolf spider	*Pardosa lugubris*		Briggs & Briggs (2004)
Wolf spiders – numerous spp	*Pisaura mirabilis* – *Lycosa* (spp)		Attenborough (2005)
European beewolf and numerous other beewolf species	*Philanthrus triangulum*		Carey (2005)

| Flora | | | |
English	Latin	Meaning	Source
Tomato	*Lycopersicon*	wolf peach	Powers (2004)
Wolf fruit	*Solanum* (spp)		Attenborough (2002)

the wolf is very varied, and includes tundra, steppe, open woodland, forest, mountain and even the fringes of farmland and settlements.

One of the ancestors of the domestic dog, the grey wolf is a powerful and muscular animal, with a thick bushy tail. The typical body is 1 to 1.4m, with tail of 30 to 48cm.[20] Males are usually larger than females. The lifespan of a wolf in the wild can be as little as four or five years, but up to nine years is not uncommon. In captivity, wolves can live much longer, from twelve to a record seventeen years.[21]

Wolves vary in colour, from almost white in the Arctic to yellowish-brown or completely black further south. Intelligent, social animals, wolves live in family groups or in packs that sometimes include more than one family or other individuals besides the core family (pls 7, 10, 11). The pack members hunt together, cooperating to run down prey such as deer, caribou and wild horses, and they also eat small animals such as mice, fish and crabs (pl. 8). Social hierarchy in the pack is well-organized and is maintained by ritualized gestures and postures – the leading male (alpha male) signalling his rank by carrying his tail higher than the others do. Pairs remain together for life.[22]

In terms of breeding, the female gives birth to three to eight pups after a gestation of about sixty-three days. Born blind and hairless, the pups venture outside the den at three weeks, and the whole pack then helps to care for and play with them.[23] The young are born in a den selected by the mother. It may be a naturally occurring hole, beneath tree roots or under a boulder, or she may have dug it herself with her strong blunt claws. The pups have huge appetites. When adults return from a successful hunt with full bellies, the pups beg, whining and wagging their tails and licking the corners of any adult's mouth until eventually it disgorges gobbets of meat from its stomach, which are then wolfed down by the pups.[24]

One of the reasons for the success of the wolf is that they will eat virtually anything (the domestic dog springs to mind here). Wolves obviously prefer large prey like deer and elk, which can feed the whole pack, but will eat worms, rodents, berries, carrion of all descriptions, fish, domestic animals and even other predators such as bears (pl. 8). Wolves in North America also hunt bison, which requires a coordinated effort, often over a number of days. This is done by constantly running the herd of bison and eventually identifying and targeting a weaker, sick or injured individual. The difficulties of hunting are such that the number of pups a pack can raise in a year is limited, and usually only the top dogs – the alpha male and alpha female – will breed. The junior members are physiologically capable of doing so, but this is prevented by aggressive behaviour from their alphas – including driving individuals out of the pack if necessary.[25]

CHAPTER 2

Archaeological evidence

INTRODUCTION

There are a number of possible ways by which wolves arrived in Ireland. The first factor to note is that they pre-date the earliest evidence of humans in Ireland by around 20,000 years. They may have survived in refugia – areas which were not covered by ice – some of which may now be offshore. They could have crossed over on the ice sheet that would have covered the northern half of the Irish Sea at least and this could easily account for their early arrival. The survival of wolves in the Arctic is evidence of their ability to survive in extremely cold conditions as long as there is suitable prey. Alternatively, it is well-established that wolves are excellent swimmers and could have swum the relatively short distance between Scotland and Ireland as they would have been able to see the land in the distance. In support of this, wolves in North America are known to cross water on ice flows and have been seen on drifting ice. When sea levels were much lower than at present, the Irish Sea would not have been the formidable barrier it is now, even though they would still have had to cross some stretches of water as no complete land bridges existed.[1]

One of the great difficulties in trying to identify wolf bones in archaeological sites in the post-glacial period is that they are very similar if not identical to early dog bones. This is not surprising, as domestic dogs are direct descendants of wild wolves and have very similar DNA. So the discussion below has relied on the assessment of various archaeological and other writers in their own judgment that certain bones were from wolves, or possibly from wolves and not domestic dogs. The earliest known record of domesticated dog occurs in the Mesolithic, one possible dog bone being found at Mount Sandel, Co. Derry. Although the bone has yet to be dated, it was found in a tightly constrained Mesolithic context.[2]

EVIDENCE FROM CAVE DEPOSITS – MOSTLY GLACIAL DATES UP TO 13,000 YEARS AGO

A lot of nineteenth- and early twentieth-century excavations were carried out in caves in which there were accumulations of bones dating back

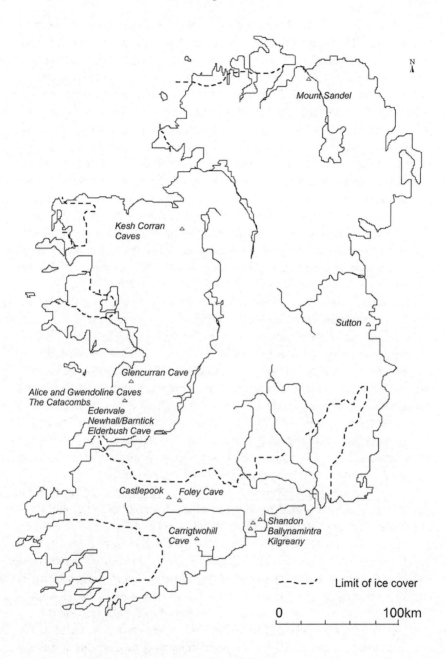

2.1 Distribution of some key archaeological wolf bone finds
(after Woodman et al., 1997; adapted by Siúbhan Comer).

thousands to tens of thousands of years, and some wolf bones were identified within many of these. Great care has to be taken when using the early reports based on those excavations, however, firstly in terms of identifying the bones and secondly in terms of the stratigraphy or context in which they were found. A lot of what was published then is now considered to be unreliable. As a result of these concerns, the Irish Quaternary Fauna Project was set up. Under the auspices of this initiative, a start was made on radiocarbon-dating the recovered cave bones. The results included early dates for many mammal species and show that the wolf was present in Ireland at least 28,000 years ago.[3] The earliest evidence comes from a series of excavated cave sites where deposits of bone accumulated over many years (fig. 2.1). These bones would have built up for a number of reasons, including the use of the caves as breeding dens for wolves and probably for respite from the severe winters. It is also likely that animals were dragged in to be eaten. The Irish wolf was first identified in Shandon and Ballinamintra Caves in Co. Waterford.[4] A mandible or jaw bone was radiocarbon-dated to 27,500±420 years BP (before present), giving the earliest confirmed date for a wolf in Ireland.[5]

The second earliest radiocarbon date for wolf bones in Ireland is from Castlepook Cave, north of Doneraile, Co. Cork.[6] This wolf mandible was eventually radiocarbon-dated to 23,470±300BP.[7] The remains of a virtually intact large probable wolf skull and a radius were recovered from deep inside Carrigtwohill Cave in Co. Cork (fig. 2.2).[8] Wolf bones from similar contexts have been found in a number of other cave sites, particularly in Shandon Cave and Kilgreany Cave in Co. Waterford and at Foley Cave, Castletownroche, Co. Cork. These discoveries indicate the presence of wolf throughout the latter part of the Midlandian Ice Age.[9]

Extensive investigations were carried out in three caves in Co. Clare in 1902.[10] The caves were Edenvale, from which 50,000 bones were extracted, and Newhall and Barntick, from which a total of 20,000 bones were removed. The identified bones included a wide variety of animals, birds and some human remains. The difficulties of clearly identifying what was wolf and what was dog were highlighted in the report, but in Barntick Cave an immature skull fragment was found which had a facial angle of forty degrees and therefore certainly belonged to a wolf, making this the first scientific discovery and identification of wolf bones in Ireland. The face angle was seen as a way of distinguishing wolf skulls from dog skulls. Other bones were categorized as 'probably wolf' and included a radius fragment and a metatarsal from Edenvale Cave. In Newhall and Barntick, the best differentiation the researchers could make resulted in sixty-nine

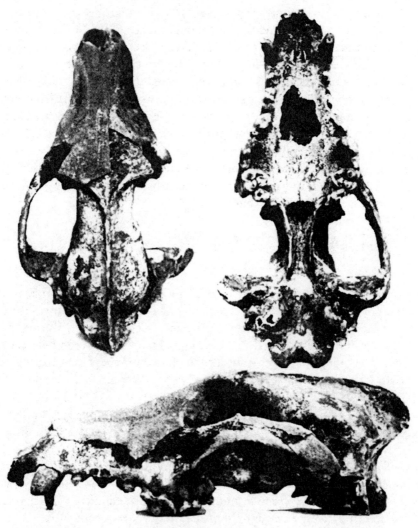

2.2 Photographs of a wolf skull recovered from Carrigtwohill Cave, Co. Cork
(after Coleman & Stelfox, 1945).

bags of 'probable dog bones', thirteen bags of 'very wolf-like bones' and
two canine teeth that had been adapted by humans as implements and
were classed as 'either dog or wolf'. Unfortunately, there was no way of
dating the bones at the time, although it is possible that some of them pre-
dated the arrival of humans in Ireland and would therefore have to be wolf
(rather than dog) bones. Dogs arrived in Ireland with humans and not
before. There is also evidence for possible wolf bones in Alice and
Gwendoline Caves and the Catacombs in Edenvale, Co. Clare.[11]

It was noted that wolves were present in Ireland during warmer phases of the last glaciation before the maximum advance of the Midlandian ice sheet around 25,000 years ago.[12] In addition, Scharff claimed that wolf bones and teeth had been found in the Kesh Caves in Co. Sligo and at Castlepook Cave in Co. Cork.[13] It must be noted that, even now, fewer than twenty-five bone-yielding caves have been excavated, in comparison with several hundred in Britain. In addition, many were poorly excavated and badly recorded.[14] So, what is known about the glacial and early post-glacial fauna is based on relatively limited evidence. In three other cave systems in Co. Clare, wolf bones were discovered by a team of excavators led by Richard Usher at the end of the nineteenth century, but they had no scientific method of dating the bones.[15]

EVIDENCE FROM POST-GLACIAL SITES – THE LAST 13,000 YEARS

In the caves on Keshcorran Hill, Co. Sligo, at an altitude of 355m, a wolf mandible dating to around 11,150±90BP was discovered.[16] Wolves were most likely present here between 10,600 and 12,000 years ago, during the last years of the giant Irish deer.[17] Late glacial faunal remains in Kilgreany Cave near Dungarvan, Co. Waterford, included wolves possibly dating to around 10,700BP, and similar results were found at Edenvale Caves, Co. Clare.[18]

At the end of the last Ice Age, man and wolf would have been in competition for the same types of prey. Gradually, associations built up between the two species. These may have originated from the capture of wolf-cubs by hunters or from their attraction to the easier pickings of human encampments. Because the social structure and behaviour patterns of a wolf pack and a group of hunter-gatherers are similar, wolves were able to fit relatively easily into human society.[19] The smaller, drier caves were used by humans as well as species such as wolves.[20] There is no doubt that the arrival of the first people into Ireland around 9,000 years ago brought them into contact with the existing wolf population, although sightings would not have been commonplace. The most likely confirmation of wolves in their surrounding area would have come from their howling at night time, which would have carried for many miles (pls 3, 7).[21]

At Mount Sandel, Co. Derry, the earliest site for human habitation so far discovered in Ireland and dating from between 9,000 and 7,500 years ago, among the very extensive fragments of burnt bones found, one has been identified as a wolf bone or possibly a bone from a domestic dog.

This would be an exceptionally early date for a domestic dog anywhere in Europe. At Lough Boora, near Birr, Co. Offaly, and dating from the same period as Mount Sandel, bones of either a wolf or a domestic dog were identified by archaeologists in the 1980s.[22] Given that wolves were widespread in Ireland in the Mesolithic and domestic dogs were rare across Europe, it is more likely that these were the bones of wolves, probably pups reared by humans. However, over the millennia, many different types of dogs have been bred from the ancestral wolf, with huge variations in function, size, temperament and physical attributes.[23] In the Irish context, the most important of these is the Irish wolf-dog or the later Irish wolfhound, which were purposely bred to aid humans in the hunting of wolves.

Traces of wolf along with other wild animals including wild boar and brown bear have been found at various Mesolithic campsites from 9,000 years ago.[24] There is very little reliable distinction between the skeletal remains of a wolf and those of a large Irish wolfhound. The angles of the eye-sockets differ between the two species, however, and this can provide a basis for differentiation, as can the dimensions of molar teeth.[25] Modern DNA methods might be able to resolve this challenge.

A shell midden from Sutton, Co. Dublin, dating from somewhere between 6,340 and 5,810 years ago, produced only a small number of mammal bones, which included one of a wolf.[26] A midden at White Park Bay, Co. Antrim, yielded one bone fragment (of a left radius) from either a dog or a wolf, but more likely the former given that the animal would have been only the size of an Irish Red Setter.[27] During the Bronze Age, wolves were still present in the landscape, especially in significant areas of woodland.[28] In the Late Bronze Age, wolves stalked the forests and were a menace to flocks of sheep in winter. At Feerwore, near Turoe in Co. Galway, the remains of what was either a wolf or a dog were identified in an Iron Age context.[29] A radius of a wolf found in Elderbush Cave in Newhall produced a radiocarbon date of 1730±60BP.[30] A recent find at Glencurran Cave in Co. Clare of a perforated tooth was possibly from a dog, a wolf or a fox.[31] The find was not in a clear archaeological context, however, and the cave contained material from the Middle and Late Bronze Ages right up to the medieval period.

The evidence for wolves in Ireland in the post-glacial period comes from a variety of excavated sites including caves, hunter-gatherer camps, loughs and middens, with post-glacial dates from sites such as Curran Point, Larne, Co. Antrim, Sutton, Co. Dublin, and stone circle K at Knockadoon, Lough Gur, Co. Limerick.[32] Wolves have been found in

2.3 Carved stone from Ardnaglass Castle, Co. Sligo, supposed to depict
a dog attacking a wolf (after Webber, 1841).

Mesolithic, Neolithic, Bronze Age, Iron Age and Early Medieval archaeological sites.[33] Possible wolf bones have been recovered from late sixth-
century contexts at Ballinderry Crannog (no. 2), Co. Offaly, and these
seem to be from one individual.[34] This may have been an animal that was
killed in a hunt and brought back to camp so the pelt could be used, or the
meat eaten; it also could have been a cub that was found and raised as a
tame animal for hunting purposes. A wooden toggle in the shape of a wolf
was recovered from a Viking Age site in Dublin.[35]

Ringforts, a common feature of the Irish landscape (there are as many
as 40,000 dotted across the country), were built partly as a defence against
wolves and to protect livestock.[36] Ringforts from the Iron Age were, in
their simplest form, cattle-pens or sheep-folds with a palisade around the
top of the bank to keep out wolves as well as thieves.[37] This type of
enclosure is still in use in parts of Eastern Europe, including Romania,
where wolves remain a threat to livestock, especially where flocks and
herds are brought up to high altitude pastures during the summer.[38] One
of the principal duties of young people and professional herders during
the summer booleying season, when cattle in particular were brought to
upland pastures, was to keep watch for wolves.[39] In Co. Tyrone, where

wolves were a great plague in the seventeenth century, they even raided the stone enclosures made to protect sheep.[40]

In contrast to these more sturdy structures, other approaches were also adopted for protection against wolves. One of the most remarkable of these was discovered between 1936 and 1951 in west Norway. Two sections of a rope fence were found to have been erected to protect sheep from straying up the mountainside towards the wild wolves near Olden in Nordefjord in the early seventeenth century. Warmer weather in the twentieth century had released the ropes from the snow and ice that had covered them since being put up by a farmer who is known to have owned the land from 1602 to 1624. This was in effect a late medieval version of a barbed wire fence.[41]

Smith, writing in 1756, stated that certain ancient enclosures had been built in Co. Kerry to secure cattle from wolves, and that the latter were not finally killed off until about 1710.[42] The evidence to support this was presentments for raising money to destroy the wolf as recorded in some old grand-jury books. The wolf was a great scourge in Ireland in former times, and it is likely that it was as protection from the wolf more so than from human enemies that the older human habitations mostly took the form of lake-dwellings (crannogs) and stockaded ringforts.[43]

Right up to late medieval times, the bawns of castles were still being used to house cattle at night for fear of human and possibly wolf predation. Furthermore, even at the end of the seventeenth century, cattle and livestock generally were liable to be carried off during cattle raids or attacked by dogs or wolves.[44] As a result, the custom of the poor was to house their animals at night in their cabin, which is similar to bringing animals into the bawn around castles and fortified houses at night. Wolves seem to have become more plentiful in Ireland in the sixteenth and seventeenth centuries because of war and famine, and it was the custom to drive cattle and sheep into special enclosures at night to protect them from wolf attack.[45] This practice is maintained in areas where wolves still occur, including parts of Spain.[46]

There is a stone plaque from Ardnaglass Castle in Skreen in Co. Sligo which currently resides in the Royal Irish Academy in Dublin and supposedly depicts a dog killing a wolf (fig. 2.3). The associated story is that

Long ago, when O Dowds were the chieftains in that part of Sligo, a wolf was wreaking havoc among the sheep in the area. In those times, most people lived on the land and there was consternation as night after night more sheep were killed by the savage wolf. What made it harder to bear was the fact that most people thought there were no longer any wolves in Ireland. O Dowd was incensed that although cleared out all around the country one wolf still lived on to destroy his sheep. He had an excellent wolf-dog, and so he released him to follow the last wolf on Ireland's shores. At first, there was a terrible chase – the O Dowd's watched from the vantage point of Ardnaglass. The chase continued, but at last O Dowd's wolf-dog was ahead and began to corner the wolf, which had tired. A savage fight between the two animals followed, and at last a great cheer rose when O Dowd's dog won the battle and the last wolf in Ireland had been eliminated. To this day, the townland where the final fight occurred is called Carrownamadoo, to commemorate the victory of the dog.[47]

Examination of the stone carving shows that it is medieval in date and clearly pre-dates the real extermination of the last wolf by several centuries.

It seems that the massive Irish wolfhound is a later medieval breed. The earliest descriptions of such a dog are from the sixteenth century and the archaeological evidence of the Early Christian period shows no dog bones larger than those of a modern German Shepherd.[48]

There is no doubt that, even with the difficulties of distinguishing wolf bones from dog bones, wolves formed a very significant part of the fauna of Ireland up to the modern period and could be found around human settlements and other archaeological sites from earliest times. It is a remarkable tribute to their adaptability that they survived right down to the late eighteenth century.

CHAPTER 3

Names

INTRODUCTION

One of the most surprising aspects of the research that was carried out for this book was the large number of references to wolves in names of all types. Initially, Irish names for wolves and those related to place-names (both in Irish and in English) seemed like the only major sources of wolf references, but it quickly became apparent that this was not the case. The search for names with wolf references broadened out to include ogham inscriptions, family names and family crests. In some cases, the wolf reference is almost hidden by being in Irish and also by the indirect way to which they are referred. Most remarkably of all, Ireland was sometimes known as 'Wolf Land' because of the number of wolves in the country long after they were gone from England.[1]

IRISH NAMES FOR THE WOLF AND THEIR EXPLANATION

There is a considerable number of names for wolves in Irish, although most are fairly obscure. By far the most common is *mac tíre* (variant and older spellings include *mactíre* and *macc tíre*). The literal translation is 'son of the country' or 'son of the land'.[2] The literal translation implies a wild animal living in and off the countryside. As will be seen below, this Irish name for wolf only occasionally appears in place-names.

The element that occurs most frequently in place-names in Irish that refer to wolves is *bréach*.[3] This has been simply translated as 'wolf'. There is some confusion in the literature because of the closeness of this word to *broc*, which means 'badger', and *breac*, which means 'speckled', as there are several place-names relating to the badger also. By careful scrutiny, these have been eliminated from the list.

One other contemporary Irish term for wolf is *faolchú*. Again, there are a number of older spellings, including *faelchu* and *fáel allaid*.[4] The literal translation here is broken down into two components: *faol*, or the older spelling *fáel*, implies 'wild', and *cú*, meaning hound. *Faol* on its own has been used in a number of Irish surnames to indicate wolf. Following on from this are terms such as *cú allaidh* and *cú allta*. These translate literally as 'wild hound', which, in turn, means wolf.[5] Associated with these variants are a whole series that start with *madra* (dog), and these are *madra alla* (variants include *madra alta*, *madra allaid* and *madra allta*).[6] These all translate literally as 'wild dog', which, of course, means wolf. Although these names for wolves do not appear in any place-names, they are quite commonly used in folklore stories that refer to wolves.

In addition to the above, there are two other names used for wolves in Irish. *Cano* means wolf cub,[7] and *glaoidheamhain* translates literally as 'wolf howler', which clearly derives from the howling of wolves.[8]

PLACE-NAMES IN IRISH, THEIR ORIGIN, EXPLANATION AND DISTRIBUTION

After looking at the many words for wolf in Irish, it is now possible to examine the place-names with a wolf component in them. It must be noted that these place-names come from every province and from eighteen of the thirty-two counties in Ireland (table 3.1). Most of the names relate to townlands.[9]

Firstly, there are ten names associated with *mac tíre* and variants. Four of these occur in Co. Wexford, including modern-day Glentire (*Cluain*

Table 3.1 Irish language 'wolf' place-names by county.

County	*Breagh*	*Mac Tíre*	*Faolchú*	Total
Clare	9	2		11
Donegal	5			5
Wexford	1	4		5
Cork	3	1		4
Armagh	3			3
Kerry	2	1		3
Mayo	3			3
Sligo	3			3
Cavan	1			1
Down			1	1
Dublin			1	1
Fermanagh	1			1
Limerick		1		1
Longford	1			1
Meath	1			1
Offaly	1			1
Tipperary		1		1

Mhic Tíre in Irish), near Enniscorthy, which is translated as 'meadow of the wolf'. The parish of Toome (*Tuaim na Mac Tíre*) in the north of the county translates as 'mound/ridge/hillock of the wolves'. In addition, two now defunct place-names are associated with wolves: Bunaskynemictiry near Kilmuckridge, which means 'bottom of the wolves gully', and Coulnemicktiry, meaning 'recess/corner of the wolves'.[10]

Knockaunvicteera in Kilmoon parish near Lisdoonvarna in Co. Clare has been translated as 'little hill of the wolf', quoting a gloss on an ancient poem in the Book of Leinster.[11] Cahermactire in Rath parish near Inchiquin Hill in the Burren has been translated as 'stone fort of the wolf'.[12] Lismakerry (*Lios Mhic Thíre*), Co. Limerick, translates as 'ring fort of the wolf'. One 'wolf' name occurs in Co. Kerry and this is Iskanamacteera in Dromod parish, which has been translated as the 'water of the wolves'.[13] One name also occurs in Co. Cork – Knockane (*Cnoc Mhic Tíre*) 'wolf hill'.[14] In Co. Tipperary, Clashavictory seems an unlikely name to have any wolf connection but in Irish its is *Clais an Mhic Tíre*, which means 'ravine of the wolf'.[15]

There are only two place-names associated with *faolchú* and variants. The best known is Feltrim Hill (Faeldruim in older Irish), Co. Dublin, which this means 'wolf ridge', with the addition of 'hill' at the end, which was then shortened to 'wolf hill'.[16] The second is Feltrim (Faeldruim), Co. Down, and this is translated as 'wolf-ridge'.[17]

All the remaining place-names in Irish are associated with *breagh* and variations, Breagh being an anglicized version of *bréach*, meaning wolf. However, there are a number of other possible meanings, so great care needs to taken. Anglicizations of Bréachmhaigh meaning 'wolf plain' or 'wolf field' can be identified. The first group of six names have a 'y' added to the end (Breaghy). Four of these townlands occur in Co. Donegal in the parishes of Clondahorky, Conwal, Donaghmore and Tullyfern, one occurs in Co. Longford in Clonbroney parish and one in Co. Armagh in Tynan parish; there is also a Breaghy Road in this location. Another group of five townlands, all in Co. Clare, are in the form of Breaghva and these occur in the parishes of Clondagad, Kilmurry, Kilrush, Moyarta and Carrigaholt. In addition, the townlands of Breaghva East and Breaghva West occur in the parish of Kilchreest, also in Co. Clare.[18]

The next variation is 'Breaghwy', a shortened version of *Bréachmhaigh*, found in Breaghwy parish in Co. Mayo and two townlands in Co. Sligo in the parishes of Ahamlish and Kilmoremoy. Two townlands in Co. Kerry have a slightly different variation – Breahig. There are a number of places called 'Breaffy', including Breaffy village and parish in Co. Sligo and

Breaffy North and Breaffy South, two townlands in Kilfarboy parish in Co. Clare. Others include Breaghey in Tynan parish in Co. Armagh, Breagho in Enniskillen, Co. Fermanagh, and Breaghna (*Bréachnach*), 'place of the wolves', in the parish of Desertserges in Co. Cork.[19] There is also Britway parish (*Bréachmhaigh*) in Co. Cork.

In terms of compound names using breagh as the source, there is a wide variety of examples associated with a range of features. Four straight-forward compound names exist, the first being Ballybreagh (*Baile Bréach*), which is translated as the 'town of the wolf' and occurs in the parish of Kilmore in Co. Armagh. The second is Breaghmore, which simply means big wolf-field or plain and occurs in the parish of Seirkeiran in Co. Offaly. Caherbreagh, which translates as the 'fort of the wolves', is located in Ballymacelligot parish in Co. Kerry. Inish-breachmhaighde, which translates as 'the island of the wolf field or plain', occurs in the parish of Templeport in Co. Cavan. This name uses a more archaic version than in most names. In Co. Meath, Ballinabrackey (*Buaile na Bréamhaí*) is translated as 'milling place of the wolf plain'.[20]

Kilbreaghy, a defunct place-name from 1618, was located near Oulart and Ballyboy in Co. Wexford. In this case, it is not clear if the 'kil' component refers to a church or a wood.[21] On Tory Island off the coast of Co. Donegal, a natural arch on a small headland is called *Pollabraher*, which has been translated by the author as 'Wolf's hole', but not with complete certainty so a question mark hangs over this name.[22]

Finally, two more unusual references to wolves in place-names occur in the parish of Kilfian in Co. Mayo.[23] The first is Breaghwyanteean, which translates as 'wolf field/plain and the fairy hill'. The second is more obscure; Breaghwyanurlaur is translated as the 'wolf field/plain of the level spot'.

This is by no means a definitive list and it is likely that there are other place-names associated with wolves, especially at townland and sub-townland level and defunct place-names. It is very likely that additional wolf references are hidden in the hundreds of place-names that contain *madra* (dog), *nagun* (of the hounds) and *con* (hound, rabbit and personal names), where a percentage of them are very likely to refer to wolves. Only after detailed work on each name would it become possible to identify whether these names were associated with wolves or not. In some cases, it may never be possible to be definitive.[24] It is also noted that cú, which is usually translated as 'hound', may also be used as a generic term that may be applied to any canine, including dog and wolf.[25]

PLACE-NAMES IN ENGLISH, THEIR ORIGIN, EXPLANATION
AND MAP OF THEIR DISTRIBUTION

In contrast to the Irish place-names associated with wolves, the English ones are concentrated in a few counties, predominantly in the province of Ulster and with a cluster in Co. Laois and Co. Offaly and one each in Co. Sligo and Co. Cork (table 3.2). The most common place-name in English which refers to wolves is Wolf Hill. The Wolfhill a few miles from Belfast, Co. Antrim, is an obvious example, but there are several others. The village of Wolfhill in Co. Laois even had a notorious shebeen called the Wolfpack, which has long been converted into a house.[26] This area was also an important staging camp during the 1798 Rebellion.[27] Wolfhill Colliery is in this parish of Rathaspick near Athy, Co. Kildare.[28] There is a townland called Wolfhill in the parish of Tamlaght O'Crilly in Co. Derry. The one English language outlier from the main distribution is Wolf Hill on Mine Road, Durrus, Bantry in Co. Cork. Wolftrap summit is in the Slieve Bloom Mountains in Cos Offaly and Laois. In 1573, this area was referred to as Wolfe Mountain.[29] In England, most of the 200 or more wolf place-names identified are associated with upland areas, but not necessarily areas linked with woodland.[30]

There are four Wolf Island place-names in Ireland. One is in Lough Gill, Co. Sligo, and is listed in Griffiths Valuation of that county. There is also a Wolf Island in the parish of Drumlane, Co. Derry, and one in Derrymacash parish in Co. Armagh.[31] In a nearby parish, but not connected to Wolf Island, is Wolf Island Bog in the Parish of Aughnagurgan, Co. Armagh.[32] The fourth example is on the Ards Peninsula in Co. Down.[33] Wolf Lough spans two parishes in Co. Fermanagh: Devenish and Enniskillen.[34] There is also a Wolf

Table 3.2 English language 'wolf' place-names, by county.

County	*Wolf Hill* *Wolftrap Summit*	*Wolf Island* *Wolf Island Bog* *Wolf Bog*	*Wolf Lough*	Total
Antrim	1	1		2
Armagh		2		2
Fermanagh			2	2
Derry	1	1		2
Cork	1			1
Down		1		1
Laois	1			1
Offaly	1			1
Sligo		1		1

Bog at Tildarg, near Ballyclare in Co. Antrim, and this is now the site of a windfarm. A number of other place-names start with 'Wolfe', which again could relate to wolves although there are difficulties with these, as outlined in the personal name section below.

OGHAM INSCRIPTIONS

Reference to wolves can be inferred from a number of ogham stones in Ireland. Ogham inscriptions occur on over 300 stones, predominantly in Ireland with a small cluster in Wales and a few in the Isle of Man and Scotland. They tend to occur in the southwest, south and east of Ireland and date from the fourth to the seventh century.[35] In this context, they pre-date most of the monastic annals, which start at the latter end of this period. The inscriptions seem to serve three functions: the first and most important of which is as monuments to named people; additionally, they were used as boundary markers, while they also indicated ownership of particular lands.[36] Ogham inscriptions were generally written in early Irish with occasional Latin and Latinized Irish names. They can consequently be very difficult to decipher, especially where the inscription is incomplete or very faint.[37]

The ogham references to wolves occur in a number of different varieties, including the word oghams of Morann Mac Main, which includes the descriptive *Conal Cuan*, translated as 'pack of wolves'.[38] A similar descriptive is *Cunagussos*, meaning 'wolf strength' or more obviously 'strength of the wolf', with *gussos* meaning strength.[39] This is more clearly translated as 'he who has the strength or vigour of a wolf'. In similar mode are *Cunamgli*, *Cun[a]netas* and *Cvnorix*, which have been literally translated as 'prince of wolves', 'champion of wolves' and 'king of wolves', but which can be more clearly interpreted as meaning 'prince/champion/ king like a wolf'.[40]

A number of compound names have also been identified, including *Gamicunas*, which is literally translated as 'winter + wolf', but which has no clear meaning. In Italy, however, the winter wolf is a common expression and is associated with seeing wolves during the worst of winter time scavenging for food near settlements. Similar problems exist with *Glasiconas*, which literally translates as 'grey + wolf' and has no obvious meaning.

It is clear from the preceding discussion that *Con* refers to a wolf, but can also mean dog or hound; *Conann* may mean wolf, but it too can refer to a hound. A diminutive form, *Cunigni* or *Cvnigni*, can also mean wolf and/or hound.[41]

Wolves were always considered good observers of the weather and when they howled and came close to settlements it was known that a storm was on its way. The Greek poet Aratus of Soli wrote:

> When through the dismal night the lone wolf howls,
> Or when at eve around the house he prowls,
> And, grown familiar, seeks to make his bed,
> Careless of man, in some outlying shed,
> Then mark! – ere thrice Aurora shall rise,
> A horrid storm will sweep the blackened skies.[42]

PERSONAL NAMES

There are a number of old Irish personal names that can be associated with wolves, but also with hounds. Whether they covered both or should only be associated with one or the other is not clear. They include, for males, Conaire, with *aire* meaning farmer/landowner, Conall, which is interpreted as meaning strong as a wolf, Conán, which is great or high wolf/hound, Conchobhar (anglicized Connor), which is interpreted as meaning wolf lover, Conn and Conri (wolf/hound with *rí*, meaning king, attached). A different root first name is Ó Faoláin, meaning wolf; the most common modern versions are Phelan and Whelan, which also appear as surnames, below.[43]

The surname Ó Conaill is common in Ireland but was originally associated especially with Co. Kerry. Conall as a personal name has been translated as 'strong as a wolf', whereas Ó Faoláin or Whelan, Whalen or Phelan has been translated as wolf, but possibly with evil connotations. The septs with this surname are primarily associated with Co. Waterford and Co. Kilkenny.[44] Kinelly is an anglicized version of Ó Cinnfhaolaidh, meaning wolf-head or learned man/leader, like an alpha male wolf presumably.

Even the indigenous surname Ó Mac Tire (son of the country = wolf) occurred in medieval times but is no longer in existence.[45] A bishop by the name of Oonahan O'Mactire, probably of Cloyne, died in 1099, and another Mactire appears in the Annals of the Four Masters as tánaiste (or heir of the chief) of Teffia. Cahermactire, a fort near Inchiquin Hill in the Burren in Co. Clare, may be named after a person, as the surname Ó Mac Tire is found in various annals.[46] A quick search of the internet turns up an individual with the surname O'Mactire in Bangladesh but clearly of European origin, and various individuals with the surname Mactire in the

USA in particular. Remarkably, there is a bagpipe band based in Albuquerque, New Mexico called the Mac-Tire of Skye, who use a wolf playing the bagpipes as their emblem and have two wolves as mascots.[47] The indigenous Ó Mac Tire name was in turn anglicized into Woulfe and Wolfe, but should not be confused with the same surname coming from an Anglo-Norman origin. Examples include Wolfeburgess East and West, near Rathkeale in Co. Limerick, Wolfestown near Rathmore in Co. Kildare and Wolfefoord in Co. Wexford, although this latter name is no longer in use (they are omitted from the list of names because of the amount of research needed to clarify the origin of each individual with one of these surnames).[48]

The surnames O Coinín and Mac Coinín, variously anglicized as Cunneen, Cunnien, Kinneen and Kenning, have usually been translated as Rabbitte, Rabbitt or Rabbette, when in fact the name actually derives from a diminutive of *cano*, a wolf cub. Confusion occurs with the later word *coinín*, meaning rabbit.[49]

To finish this section with a couple of examples of the Wolf surname in Ireland, Nicholas Wolf of Limerick was a native merchant who traded via Limerick and Waterford with Bristol in December 1585,[50] while in the 1940s or 1950s, the appropriately named Billy Wolf was a gamekeeper in the parish of Breaffy (a name that means 'plain of the wolf').[51]

HERALDIC CRESTS

Wolves were a common feature on heraldic crests and occur throughout many European countries including England, Scotland, France, Spain, Germany and Italy. English individuals and families with wolves on their crests include Sir Charles Lupus, from the mid-fourteenth century, Viscount Wolseley and the Lovetts, Lows and Lovells.[52]

It must be noted that a wide variety of beasts, including mythical creatures, are used in heraldic symbolism, so their association with particular families has to be viewed carefully. The use of the wolf as a heraldic symbol denoted men who served their countries and were both fierce and treacherous. Crossly also describes them as truce-breakers.[53] The wolf was also used to indicate perseverance, either in siege or in effort.

The heraldic crest of the O'Callaghan family shows a wolf heading from a clump of trees, while the O'Crean crest consists of a wolf upright on its hind legs on the main crest and a half-wolf on the helmet crest. The heraldic crest of the O'Quins is a wolf's head.[54]

CHAPTER 4

Mythology, folklore and superstitions

INTRODUCTION

A number of categories of the folklore of wolves in Ireland have been identified.[1] These are: wolves in Ireland in former times; stories of their depredations; steps taken to protect livestock from them; wolves captured; wolf fights man or animal; wolf's gratitude to man's kindness; and the capture or killing of the last wolf in the district, barony, county, province or Ireland as a whole.

Of all the animals, the wolf is perhaps the most feared in terms of superstition, being a favourite disguise of the Devil and everywhere linked with evil, just like the snake.[2] This is clearly shown in the illustration of a wolf with an evil-looking tail in the Book of Kells (pl. 5). Many warrior groups throughout history used wolfskins as part of their uniform, including the Romans, the Vikings and many North American tribes, both to show their strength to their opponents and to inspire themselves in battle.[3]

According to Welsh legend, the wolf was created not by God but by the Devil, and the creature has retained its association with evil ever since, being blamed for attacking livestock and humans, although curiously enough, it is also said to fear crabs and shrimps.[4] The wolf was used in many medieval works to represent the Devil in the Christian tradition and, like snakes, it was an easy one to use to get the religious message across to peasant people in particular, who had little formal knowledge, but had a very good understanding of the natural world and the way it operates throughout the year.[5] This was emphasized during the worst ravages of the Black Death in the fourteenth century, when wolves were seen to feed on the corpses of the dead.

Many European children's stories, including those going back as far as Aesop's Fables and, for example, Little Red Riding Hood (which probably dates back to the seventeenth century at least) include the dangerous wolf. These stories were told to warn children of the dangers of wolves and the forest in which they were often found.[6] Phrases like 'a wolf in sheep's clothing' have entered the vernacular as a result of these stories, all of course depicting the wolf in a bad light. In addition, wolves were associated with fairies in the Germanic tradition, but little has been identified in this context from Ireland so far.

WOLVES IN ANCIENT IRISH MYTHS AND LEGENDS

At the end of the ancient story of Diarmuid and Grainne, following the death of Diarmuid, Grainne took refuge on *Sliabh na mBan* (Slievenamon in Co. Tipperary), in order to give birth to a son and to escape persecution. After her unnamed son was born, a problem developed with a wolf that was in the habit of coming into the camp and helping itself to the food that was available. Eventually, Grainne asked another son to help, otherwise they might starve. The next time the wolf appeared in the campsite, the son grabbed the wolf by the throat and held it half-strangled until his mother returned when, presumably, she killed it.[7]

During the reign of King Conn, a smith's daughter found she was pregnant by the defeated and presumed dead King Cormac and went out into the woods to give birth, aided by a mid-wife. After she gave birth to a son, a belt naming him for King Cormac was put around his waist. A she-wolf then appeared and took the child away as the two women fainted. The wolf raised the boy along with her three cubs in a cave and, as time went by, she cared more for the boy than for her own cubs. By the age of 1½ years, the boy and the cubs could be found playing in the woods outside the den. They were eventually spotted by some hunters who managed to catch the naked boy; it was only then they noticed the belt around the child and the inscription on the belt. The child was given to a nobleman to raise. As the child grew, he got the name Son of the Wolf, which he despised, but when he was older he was finally told about his discovery in the woods with a she-wolf.[8] This story has some of the elements of many classical myths about wolves raising future heroes; for example, Remus and Romulus, the founders of Rome. It is a motif that occurs in Irish folklore usually under the guise of 'future hero found in wolf den'.[9]

A contemporary of *Cúchullain* named *Conall Cairnech* was hunted by three red wolves of the Martini.[10] Wolves commonly interacted with the Fianna, a band of warriors who used to hunt the wolves at night.[11] William Butler Yeats was interested in the Fianna and, for a printing of his poem 'Inisfree', he was depicted dressed up as an Irish warrior complete with wolfskin. This is reminiscent of many North American Indians, who also used wolfskins. In the *Táin Bó Cúailnge*, *Cú Chullain* is threatened by the daughter of King *Búan* the Constant after he rebuffs her advances. She threatens to turn into a she-wolf and stampede his cattle towards him, which she does later. Further on in the story, the expression 'into exile to dwell among the wolves and foxes' is used.[12] Bran, one of the hounds of *Cú Chullain*, was described as having a number of remarkable features, including being dark green with black sides and blood-red ears … a small head, white breast, dragon's eyes, wolf's claws, lion's vigour and a serpent's venom. Even more bizarrely, Bran was also his nephew, as his sister had been turned into a female dog and had given birth to two hounds. This explains the very unusual nature of the hounds.[13] *Cú Chullain* and another of the Fianna, *Caoilte*, were said to love to hear wolves howl and went so far as to describe it as music. Cormac's Glossary describes the howling of wolves as uplifting.[14]

Mac Cecht was said to have killed a wolf that was feeding on a living woman on a battlefield.[15] Cormac mac Airt, who, like Romulus and Remus, was said to have been raised by a she-wolf and was eventually rescued, could understand their speech and four wolves accompanied him into his battle and rebellion against Lugaid mac Con. These wolves also accompanied him for the rest of his life. On his way to his foster-father, it was said that the party was attacked by wolves but that wild horses drove them off.[16] Queen Maedhbh was described as a fair-haired wolf-queen.[17]

Wolf motifs appear in Celtic art from across Europe. North Gaulish coins, for instance, depict the wolf eating the sun. This wolf symbolism has a possible link with an early Norse myth of the world's creation, fall and renewal, where the end of the world is signified by the wolf's attack on the sun and moon. Wolves are common in Norse mythology, particularly in association with the god Odin, who was devoured by the wolf Fenrir despite the fact that he had two wolf companions that were Geri (hungry) and Freki (ravenous).[18] The Greeks referred to the volcanic gases that came out of the ground as wolves, and the temple of Apollo in Athens was called the Lyceum, which means wolfskin. The wolf also features in Chinese mythology associated with astronomy. Wolves feature heavily in the mythology of the indigenous tribes of North America. Rome of course was founded by Romulus and Remus who were reared by a she-wolf and are celebrated in the festival of Lupercalia. Similar myths occur in Turkey, where wolves were believed to have sired the nation.[19]

Depictions of wolves as battle symbols and on war-gear also occur and these are directly associated with ferocity and aggression and may indicate symbolic potency. Wolf decorations were also used on war-trumpets. Depictions of wolves by Celtic artists were not uncommon, along with mythical and other real animals and plants. Occasionally, artists would combine two or more animals and humans. The Tarasque of Noves, a stone carving from France dating to the third or second century BC, is a statue 1.12m high which consists of a half-lion/half-wolf monster with a human bone in its mouth and front paws gripping two human heads with their eyes closed in death.[20] A wide range of animals are represented in early illuminated manuscripts, metalwork and stone carvings and this continues the Celtic tradition. These depictions occasionally include wolves, as in the Book of Kells. These depictions can be realistic or include distortion to fantastical representations.[21]

The eighth-century tale *Togail Bruidne Da Derga* notes that King Conaire kept seven wolves as hostages in his house in order to ensure that the wolves of Ireland only took one male calf from each herd each year.[22] An old Irish saga telling of events associated with the possible reign of King Cormac Mac Airt (AD227–266) and written in the eleventh century in what is known as the Book of Leacain, includes a ransom for Fionn MacCumhaill consisting of two of all the main creatures of Ireland, including wolves.[23] This has obviously hints of the Noah story in the Bible, with two of all creatures being saved.

In the legend of the cave of *Cruachain*, Connacht, the entrance to the otherworld also known as the Irish entrance to Hell, one of the individuals to come out of this populous cave was *Olc Aí*, known as an otherworld figure whose name *Olc* has wolfish connotations.[24] This also shows how wolves, which would breed in caves and were seen going into and out of them, were seen as entering and exiting the underworld.

WOLF ENCOUNTERS IN THE LIVES OF IRISH SAINTS

When St Patrick was a shepherd boy in Ireland, a wolf carried off one of the sheep he was looking after, returning the following day with the sheep still alive and laying it unharmed at the saint's feet. St Patrick was also said to have punished the king of Wales, Vereticus, by turning him into a wolf. St Colman had a covenant with the local wolves that they would not draw blood from anyone.[25] In a marginal gloss in the Martyrology of Aengus, at 3 September, a name is explained as *Doire-na-con*, the oak-wood in which were formerly wild dogs and she-wolves used to dwell therein.[26]

In the Annals of Clonmacnoise for AD688 there is a reference to a wolf speaking with a human voice.[27] In his life of Molaise (St Laisren), some fifty years after his death, among other strange occurrences the wolf was heard to speak with a human voice, which was horrific to all.[28] It is possible that Giraldus Cambrensis was referring to these stories when he

4.1 Depictions of a priest talking to a wolf, and a lone wolf (after Cambrensis, 1188).

mentioned the story of a wolf speaking to a priest (fig. 4.1).[29] However, a far more elaborate story of people being forced to take the form of wolves (see below) notes that wolves and foxes were the only beasts to be considered harmful, but suggest the mouse as a third.[30]

A Latin life of St Canice describes how a wolf ate a calf from each of two cows. The owner bewailed the loss of the calf to St Canice, who told him to return to his cows and clap his hands. When he did so, the wolf returned and put its head into the calf-tie or halter. Miraculously, the cows treated the wolf as their calf and licked it as they were being milked. The wolf continued to return at morning and evening milking-times for this purpose until the end of the season. The importance of the calf and ultimately the wolf in this tale is the need to keep the cow producing milk for as long as possible, hence the wolf taking the place of the calf.[31]

Another saint associated with wolves was St Mo Lua. He was credited with providing a cooked calf in the monastic guest house for a pack of hungry wolves on which he had taken pity. This occurred each year and, as a result of their gratitude, the wolf-pack took on the responsibility of protecting the monastic livestock from other wolves and robbers.[32] Stories of wolves helping people in trouble and adopting infants occur in many parts of the world and somewhat belie the view of them just being evil.[33]

Columbanus was known as a *cú glas* or grey wolf.[34] Many stories refer to the closeness of wolves to saints. Wolves would come out of the woods to lick the feet of St Colman as any dog would do. St Caoimhghin and St Maodhog were said to have fed starving wolves from their flocks.[35] These stories are commonly associated with many saints across Europe.

Some further details are added to this story, explaining that a curse was given by St Natalis, a disciple of St Patrick and the founder and abbot of Kilmanagh near Kilkenny.[36] Others say it was St Patrick himself who cursed the people, after they refused to listen to him preach but bayed at him like wolves. In addition, the wolfmen of Ossory only attacked sheep and cattle and not men and thus were true wolves in their nature, whereas the werewolves of other countries were devourers of human flesh and attacked humans. The wolfmen were working out their saintly punishment and were not the evil monstrous beings found in other countries.

A similar curse is also attributed to St Nathy (St Nath-Í) who set up a bishopric in Achonry, Co. Sligo, and who cursed a family so that every member had to transform into a wolf once every seven years and live on the blood of their relations.[37] Although the names of the two saints are similar, they come from different times and different parts of the country. St Natalis died in AD563 whereas St Nathy was a seventh-century saint. The wolf clearly occupied a special place in the literature of the early Irish saints.[38] On the Continent, the best known story of this type is about St Francis of Assisi and the Gubbio wolf in the late twelfth/early thirteenth century. St Francis negotiates with the wolf to prevent him from further attacks on humans and livestock, the deal being sealed with a paw shake.[39]

WOLF REFERENCES IN THE BREHON LAWS

The Brehon Laws were an ancient system of laws used by the Irish as a basis for their legal system. They were in use right up to the later Middle Ages. Wolves were one of only three wild mammals (fox and red deer were the other two) considered as pets according to the *Bretha Comaithchesa* ('The judgments of neighbourhood', a legal tract considered vital to good management of mixed farming and for good relationships between neighbours).[40] The early Irish law texts state that along with heron, deer and foxes, wolves were kept as pets by the Irish.[41] In addition, any offences committed by the pet wolf were to be charged at the same rate as those of the domestic dog. These offences would include attacks on humans and domestic animals. Particular legal complications arose when a domestic dog and a wolf together kill a young sheep. If it is known that a wolf pack is present in a location, it is illegal for a person to drive his neighbour's livestock near them and he must pay compensation if he does and if there are any loses.[42]

The law texts do not appear to regard the wolf as being of direct danger to humans, and this would be in line with modern zoological thinking, which holds that attacks on humans are very rare and are carried out by sick, old or rabid individuals.[43] It was considered taboo for humans to eat marrow from deer bones that had been gnawed by wolves.[44]

WOLVES IN MORE RECENT FOLKLORE

In times gone by, the mere sight of a wolf was supposed to be enough to render a man dumb,[45] assuming the wolf saw the man first, and even saying the word 'wolf' risked an imminent encounter with one, according to Pliny.[46] Plutarch recorded that a wolf's breath was so hot that it could soften and even melt any sort of bone.[47]

An obscure legal passage suggests that an especially powerful and aggressive ox might be capable of defending the herd; this ox was known as the *dam conchaid*, which can be translated as the 'wolf-fighting ox'. In addition, a Middle Irish poem refers to a brindled bull which protected its herd from wolves and other dangers.[48]

Fergus Kelly was unable to find any references in the written sources of the early period to the hunting of wolves by dogs in Ireland.[49] It seems, therefore, that the massive Irish wolfhound is a later breed. The earliest descriptions of such a dog are from the sixteenth century and the archaeological evidence of the Early Christian period shows no dog bones larger than those of a modern Alsatian. Using as a source a captain in General Ireton's regiment, he noted that the slaughtered garrison of Cashel in 1647 included a number of Irishmen with tails. No wonder the idea of the Irish wolf-men survived and entered popular legend![50]

A quote from an anonymous manuscript dated 1683 and describing Co. Kildare states that

> Such is their opinion of souls departed that as the party was conditioned when alive his soul is transmigrated into some creature of like fierce disposition as a cruel man into a wolf and the like, hence the first lamb or calf that fall in that season they devote or dedicate to him and call or term him their gossip, having thus cajoled him as they think they suppose he'll spare their herd or flock that year; and some will have the name imports so much mac-tere.

A later commentator added: 'Read mactíre (which is son of that country) or one of their own people, but these creatures being near destroyed they will not be used'.[51]

The wild Irish pray for wolves and wish them well and then they are not afraid to be hurt by them.[52] Wolves are often associated with the full moon; for example, a German book states that the wild Irish have a custom that when the moon is new they squat upon their knees and pray to the moon that it may leave them vigorous and healthy, as it has found them, and they request particularly that they may be safe from wolves.[53]

In the Poitou region of France, the magpie was honoured by bunches of heather and laurel tied to treetops because it gave warning by its chattering of the approach of wolves.[54] The magpie is possibly a recent arrival to Ireland, a flock of them being blown across the Irish Sea from Britain to Wexford in a storm in 1684, and so this linkage between the two species had no real time to develop here, as wolves were already becoming rarer in Ireland at that time.

A number of interesting stories relating to wolves in Ireland give an impression of the menace of wolves, particularly in or near forested locations. One account in particular is worth quoting at length:

> My father, whose youth was spent in Ireland, and who died twenty one years ago [1841], at the age of seventy-four [b. 1767], could tell many very interesting anecdotes (related to himself by uncles and aunts on his mother's side) connected with the ravages of wolves in that country, in the days when these animals were very formidable there. Some of these accounts are but indistinctly remembered by me; but it was a source of wonder and amusement in early childhood to hear them told by my dear father on a winter's evening. There are one or two very clearly impressed on my memory; and, as the race is now extinct in the British Isles, it may possibly interest the present and coming generations to have them recorded. An ancestor of my father's family led the humble yet pleasant life of a woodcutter, living in a little habitation at some distance from the scene of his labours. He possessed one of those noble and beautiful animals, now also nearly or quite extinct, the Irish wolf-dog – Turnbull by name – an almost necessary protection in that day, when a thickly wooded country afforded abundant shelter for those ferocious masters of the forest, which, even singly, would attack men, and sometimes visit the cottages, and watch their opportunity to carry off young children. Malone (for that I believe was the man's name) went out to his work

one day incautiously unprotected by his faithful dog. He worked later than usual that evening, and towards the close of his day's labour, when he had bound up many faggots of fallen wood, a large and savage wolf issued from the thicker part of the forest and made directly towards him, seeing, no doubt, that he was unarmed and alone. Malone immediately pulled one of the thickest stakes from a bundle of wood and prepared to make the best defence in his power, warding off the attacks of the furious brute, and walking backwards towards home, well knowing that to turn his back to the enemy would be immediately fatal. He also thought that his good friend Turnbull might be just within hearing, and had the presence of mind to call out repeatedly, at the top of his voice, 'Turnbull! Turnbull!' Now, it so happened that his wife at home felt a little anxious; and the more so, seeing that the dog, instead of being with his master, was lying comfortably asleep before the embers of the hearth. She went out, therefore, to try if she could see or hear anything of her husband, and stood, earnestly watching, on the top of a little hill near the house, when the distant call came upon her ear. In haste, she descended, guessing well the nature of the impending danger, and taking the dog to the same spot, she made him stand beside her, gently patting him that he might be still and listen. In a few moments, the faithful animal heard – as his mistress had done, and now a little nearer – the well-known call 'Turnbull! Turnbull!' No more was needed: the dog instantly darted off at his utmost speed, and was soon lost to the sight of the trembling wife, who gazed after him, riveted, as it were, to the spot where she stood. It need hardly be said how thankful the poor man was to hear his bounding step, nor how quickly the cruel enemy fled on seeing his antagonist approaching. Turnbull, however, followed up the chase, and it was some time before he returned, bearing abundant evidence, in his wounded and blood-stained appearance, what a conflict had taken place between him and the wolf, and leaving little doubt that he had been the victor.

Another case my father related, in which a wolf, taking up a little child by its clothes, was carrying it off as fast as such a heavy load would allow him. The child, just old enough to speak, and possibly having been accustomed to be played with, or even thus carried, by one of the large dogs, thought it very nice, and enjoying the ride, exclaimed in the Irish language 'I'm a-going!', repeating the words in a singing tone until rescued from its perilous situation by its parents, who were in time to follow and bring back their darling in safety.

One more instance I remember, in which several wolves attacked one of the Malone family, when returning from a journey on horseback, one dark night. He put spurs to his terrified steed, but the wolves were close behind, and actually made several leaps to the horse's hind quarters, inflicting severe wounds with their fangs. The traveller just reached his own door, however, himself unhurt, though frightened almost out if his senses, exclaiming to his brother at home 'Oh! James, James let me in – my horse is ate with the wolves!'[55]

However embellished over time, these stories are possibly based on actual encounters with wolves, as the dating would suggest an early 1700s date and probably earlier, when wolves were still found throughout Ireland.

One way to protect yourself and your horse is with music; a fiddle or bagpipe was known to scare away wolves.[56] This information possibly originates in a story recorded in a letter in 1624:

A pleasant tale I heard Sir Thomas Fairfax relate of a soldier in Ireland, who having got his passport to go for England, as he passed through a wood with his knapsack upon his back, being weary, he sat down under a tree where he opened his knapsack and fell to some victuals he had; but upon a sudden he was surprised with two or three wolves, who, coming towards him, he threw them scraps of bread and cheese till all was done; then the wolves making a nearer approach unto him, he knew not what shift to make, but by taking a pair of bagpipes which he had, and as soon as he began to play upon them, the wolves ran all away as if they had been scared out of their wits. Whereupon the soldier said 'A pox take you all, if I had known you had loved music so well, you should have had it before dinner'.[57]

Two stories of wolves in Co. Mayo survive from 1745.[58] One concerns the last wolf in the county, which was killed in that year in the parish of Kilgeevar near Louisburgh. A man walking from Roonith to Drummin and Aughagower, having traversed the most dangerous part of his journey securely, met an acquaintance at Cregganbaun and, thinking that the danger was past, gave him his dagger, only to be killed by a wolf further on. The second story from the same area tells of a wolf coming to dry himself by the fire in a bothy. A man in his bed hid under the blanket. The wolf jumped on the bed, but the man managed to throw the blanket over the wolf and, after a struggle, he killed it. Both stories should be treated with some scepticism, however, particularly in the latter case, where versions of this story exist in which the animal involved is a wild cat, which in an Irish context is either a feral domestic cat or a pine marten.[59]

The fox outwitting the wolf is a common enough theme in Irish folklore:

> A fox and a wolf went off one time to rob a fowl house. They ate their way in through the wall of the house and then began to kill the fowl and drink their blood. After a while, the fox went out and came in again. 'Where are you now', says the wolf. 'Oh', says the fox, 'I went out to see if the farmer was coming'. '*Muise mo thruagh thu*' [I pity you], says the wolf, 'what delay will we have in escaping the way we came in when we hear him coming'. So they ate again and after another time the fox went out again and came in. Very soon after, he left again and this time he didn't come back but stayed outside. He asked the wolf several times to come out, but he was too greedy to come. Finally, the farmer came along, and when the wolf went to go he got stuck in the hole, for he had too much eaten. The fox was measuring himself every time he went in and out and wasn't looking out for the farmer, and when he realized that he couldn't afford to eat any more he stayed outside. It took no time for the farmer to get the spade and work it on the wolf's head.[60]

The wolf as the devil is another common theme, showing the links between wolves and evil and demonic forces. However, somewhat contrary to this, stories of the wolf's gratitude for human kindness also occur.[61] This also appears in the lives of the Irish saints and their dealings with wolves. Other wolf themes include children being reared by wolves, which of course has echoes of Romulus and Remus and even modern claims of a similar nature. The killing of children by wolves is a recurring theme that contrasts with the previous group of stories. Another subject that crops up is the tricking of wolves to carry out tasks like ploughing, among many others.

Even more remarkable is the tradition that there were dwarf wolves on Achill Island. It is claimed that they were common as late as 1904 and were still in existence as late as 1920.[62] In support of their claim, Cunningham and Coghlan refer to other so-called dwarf wolf species around the world, including the Japanese wolf (now extinct) and the Falkland Islands Dog (*Dusicyon australis*) (also extinct), and they highlight the fact that many of these are associated with islands. In fact, however, the Japanese wolf consisted of two sub-species of the grey wolf, with one being slightly bigger than the other, but both being considered somewhat smaller than the grey wolf itself; hence their dwarf-like stature. In the case of the Falkland Islands Dog, little is known of its origin but it could only have got to the islands with the help of humans. It is most likely related to unknown or extinct South American canids and is not considered a member of the wolf family at present. A realistic explanation for the Achill Island animals is that what was being described was a local breed of dog called the cordog, which is no longer in existence and was a cross between collie and a terrier.[63]

If there truly were dwarf-wolves on Achill Island, then this would have been one of the biggest zoological discoveries in Europe in at least one hundred years. Given the recent identification of a new species of wolf in Ethiopia and ongoing problems in identifying the origin of the Falkland Islands Dog, we clearly have a lot of unfinished work to be done on canids from around the world.

Even today, some customs survive concerning wolves. At a funeral at the Gate Cemetery, Ogonnelloe, Killaloe, Co. Clare, in 2002, an interesting ritual was still being undertaken in relation to wolves.[64] The cemetery was old and walled and located in the centre of a field. The mourners carried the coffin around the cemetery and placed it on the ground at the entrance to the cemetery. The old custom was to place the coffin three times on the ground outside the walls of the cemetery, so that the wolves would not know where the corpse was buried. Apparently this was a custom that had been revived in 1939 after some time. Across the Shannon in Temple Kelly (also known as Temple Hollow) in Ballina, north Tipperary, this custom is also prevalent.[65] In nearby Quin, Co. Clare, it was the custom to use two coffins, one empty and one full in order to cause confusion and also to hide the bodies from the devil. These burial traditions rather gruesomely suggest that there was a fear that wolves might disturb new graves in their search for food. By placing the coffin on the ground the wolves would be confused as to where the body was interred, as the scent would be scattered. Further evidence of this concern comes from the Highlands of Scotland, where it was the custom to bury the dead on offshore islands in the 1500s for fear that the hungry wolves would dig up and eat the corpses.[66] In the Midlands of England around AD500 it is noted that a branch from a tree was laid over the dead body to stop wolves or forest dogs from digging it up.[67]

REFERENCES TO IRISH WOLVES IN LITERARY WORKS

A limited analysis of some early nature poems revealed two mentions of wolves.[68] Mad Sweeney in 'Suibhne Geilt' mentioned that he lived in the company of wolves and, on his deathbed, wrote a poem which has two references to wolves:

> More melodious to me once
> Was the yelping of the wolves
> Than the voice of a cleric indoors
> a-baaing and a-bleating
>
> Fox cubs scampering
> Close to me in their play
> Wolves to the kill scrambling
> Their sound drives me away.[69]

Fynes Moryson, who was in Ireland during the 1590s and also between 1600 and 1603 as personal secretary to Lord Mountjoy, head of government and commander-in-chief of the crown army in Ireland, is credited with a cynical Latin verse about Ireland:

> For four vile beasts Ireland hath no fence:
> Their bodies lice, their houses rats possess;
> Most wicked priests govern their conscience.
> And ravening wolves do waste their fields no less.[70]

The 1581 poem 'Dirge of the Munster Forest' by Emily Lawless uses a reference to wolves in the refrain:

> On the grey wolf I lay my sovereign ban,
> The great grey wolf who scrapes the earth away;
> Lest, with hooked claw and furious hunger, he
> Lay bare my dead for gloating foes to see –
> Lay bare my dead, who died, and died for me.[71]

One of the most surprising aspects of the survival of large number of wolves in Ireland long after they had been exterminated in England and Wales is that the country became known as 'wolf-land'.[72] This was partly due to the letters and other communications from the new Cromwellian settlers in Ireland and soldiers who had fought in Ireland filtering back to England describing the widespread presence of wolves in Ireland and occasional encounters with them. They were described as a menace.

The poem on the 1692 Battle of La Hogue, called 'Advice to a painter' and written by Savile and Marwell, includes the line 'A chilling damp and wolf-land howl runs through the rising camp'.[73] Macaulay quotes a poem published in 1719 to prove that wolves were quite common in Munster at that date.[74] A poem of 1719 entitled 'McDermott, or the Irish fortune hunter' suggests that wolf-killing was a popular sport in Munster:

> It happen'd on a day with horn and hounds,
> A baron gallop'd through MacDermot's grounds,
> Well hors'd, pursuing o'er the dusty plain
> A wolf that sought the neighbouring woods to gain:
> Mac hears th' alarm, and, with his oaken spear,
> Joins in the chase, and runs before the peer,
> Outstrips the huntsman, dogs, and panting steeds,
> And, struck by him, the falling savage bleeds.[75]

In William Shakespeare's play *As You Like It* (Act 5: Scene 2), Rosalind says 'Pray you, no more of this; 'tis like the howling of Irish wolves against the moon'.[76] John Derrick also notes the existence of Irish wolves in his *Image of Ireland*: 'No beastes (I saie) which do possess one jote of crewel kinde, except the wolfe that noisome is, in Irish soile I find'.[77] William Dammerell, in a poem called 'The hound of the heroes' about the exploits of the might of Irish wolf-dogs, sometimes called slaughter dogs during Roman times, states in the fourth verse:

> The elk of old Erin
> You brought to his knees
> At the roar of your challenge
> The timber wolf flees.[78]

With his poetry much rooted in the rural landscape of Ireland, Seamus Heaney's poem 'Midnight' describes wolves as 'panting, lolling, vapouring'.[79]

THE USE OF WOLF PARTS IN MEDICINE AND AS MEDICAL
CHARMS

A number of medicines made from wolf parts, including organs, were used to treat a wide variety of illnesses in the 1700s.[80] For example, two ounces of the lungs pulverized and mixed with honey and drunk in cow's milk cure an illness of the lungs, coughs and shortness of breath. Powdered wolf liver drunk in sweet milk was considered to cure consumption, coughs and obstructions of the liver. The heart pulverized and drunk in 'piony water' was used to treat epilepsy. Gall mixed with honey was used to treat ailments of the eyes. Even the dung of a wolf was considered useful and when ground was used to combat colic.

Oil extracted from the wolf was viewed as a powerful remedy against gout; the oil was rubbed onto the affected parts. Wolf fat mixed with aniseed oil was used for treating aches and pains, and parts affected by gout. The guts washed in wine, dried in an earthen pot in an oven, and drunk with white wine was another cure for the colic. It was claimed that a wolf's tooth was 'better than coral' for children's teeth.[81] It is not clear what the wolf's tooth actually does, but the description shows the wide variety of uses for wolf parts in medicine, much the same as traditional Chinese medicine uses parts of many species of animals.

A band of the fresh skin of a wolf worn round the body as a girdle was recommended as a treatment for falling sickness (epilepsy) and rabies.[82] A slightly different version goes on to state that wrapping sufferers from epilepsy in a wolfskin will safeguard them from fits.[83] In some parts of Europe, wolfskins were also reputed to keep the house free of flies. Wolves' teeth were rubbed against the gums to relieve toothache in the young and, in France, were worn around the necks of young children to safeguard them against evil.[84]

Hanging a wolf's tail over a barn door will keep other wolves away, and eating a dish of wolf meat would prevent a person from seeing ghosts. Sleeping with a wolf's head under the pillow will apparently ward off nightmares.[85] This idea dates to the fifth century BC and was first written down by Sextus Placitius in his book *Medicina de quadrupedibus*. Wolf heads were also supposed to give courage according to an old Sicilian belief, and wolf heads were also used as a charm against rabies. It was very bad misfortune to step on a dead wolf, as it caused a person to lose the use of their legs. A horse was said to go lame if it stepped on a wolf track.[86]

Another charm was to hammer two stones against each other in order to ward off the wolves. This practice is depicted in a medieval bestiary. It is interesting to note that in Shakespeare's *Macbeth*, the three witches included tooth of wolf as part of their concoction.[87] In some parts of Saxon England, around AD500, it was considered taboo to use the word 'bear' and the term 'bee-wolf' was used instead; indeed, this may even be the source of the name Beowulf.[88]

In his commentary on his atlas on Ireland, John Speed states that

Wolves they did make their God-sibs, terming them Chari Chriss and so thought themselves preserved from their hurts ... about childrens necks they hung the beginning of St John's Gospell, a crooked naile of an horishow, or a peece of a wolves skin.[89]

The first part, although obscure, implies that wolves were made god-brothers or -sisters to children and this preserved them from attack from wolves. The second part is more straightforward, in that a piece of wolfskin was used as a charm to protect the child. Writing in 1585, William Camden referred to the wolves as gossips, calling them Chari Christ.[90]

There was a belief that wolves' teeth were lucky and kept off evil. A letter from Lady Wentworth to her son Lord Stafford, written in 1713, notes that she had 'made your daughter a present of a wolf's tooth. I sent to Ireland for it and set it here in gold. They are very lucky things; for my twoe first, one did dye, the other bred his very ill, and none of ye rest did, for I had one for all the rest'.[91] The remarkable aspect of this letter is that Lady Wentworth attributed the loss of one of her children to the lack of a wolf's tooth and the survival of the others due to the possession of a wolf's tooth. This is in keeping with some North American and other cultures, in which wolf magic can be potentially both harming and healing. Pieces of wolfskin and hair were worn by warriors to ward off injury and death, and infants were fed pieces of wolf heart in the hope that they would become brave and fearless warriors. The Vikings also wore wolf coats and drank wolf blood before battle in order to give them strength and courage. In an illustration for the printing of 'Inisfree', Jack Yeats depicts his brother W.B. Yeats dressed up as an ancient Irish warrior complete with wolfskin.[92] Wolf liver was a common enough medicine in parts of pre-Columbian Mexico and Europe in the Middle Ages. Dried wolf meat was even eaten to cure sore shins and Roman women attended the festival of Lupercalia in the hope of increasing their fertility.[93]

THE BELIEF THAT SOME IRISH COULD CHANGE INTO WOLVES AND WEREWOLVES

It has been suggested that the legend of the werewolf developed from the terror of man-eating wolves during frequent attacks on humans associated with the downturn in climate in the early fifteenth century.[94] Descriptions of werewolves from that time referred to humans covered in hair, with clawed hands and small, flat, pointed ears. It was also briefly noted that some humans could at will take the shape of wolves and become werewolves.[95] The story of werewolves goes much further back, to Ancient Greece.[96] There is a vast literature on werewolves, and the material relevant to Ireland is discussed below.

The ancient Celts were supposed to be able to change themselves into wolves. Some accounts say that they left their own human bodies in the care of their friends, because if anything happened to the body they would be in wolf form forever. The idea that someone would deliberately take on an animal form is shared with many ancient cultures, including some native North Americans, who believed they would gain insight and abilities from such animal transformations.[97] The Greeks believed that anyone who eats meat from a lamb that was killed by a wolf would turn into a vampire.[98]

There is also a much older pan-European superstition, especially in France, that men in certain circumstances could change into wolves and then hunt down and feed on human prey.[99] There were certain physical characteristics that made a person more likely to turn into a werewolf, and prime candidates were those born out of wedlock or on Christmas Eve or anyone who had unusually hairy hands and flat fingers (that is, paw-like) or eyebrows that meet over the nose. It has been suggested that some people could control their transformation, becoming wolves on donning wolfskin coats or belts.[1]

Here is an example of a detailed early Irish story which supposedly dates to the 1160s:

> A priest was on a journey and had for company only a little boy. A wolf came up to them and immediately broke into these words: 'Do not be afraid! Do not fear! Do not worry! There is nothing to fear!' They were completely astounded and in great consternation. The wolf then said some things about God that seemed reasonable. The priest called on him and adjured him by the omnipotent God and faith in the Trinity not to harm them and to tell them what kind of creature he was, who, although in the form of a beast, could speak human words. The wolf gave a Catholic answer in all things and at length added: 'We are natives of Ossory. From there every seven years, because of the imprecation of a certain saint, namely the abbot Natalis, two persons, a man and a woman, are compelled to go into exile not only from their territory but also their bodily shape. They put off the form of man completely and put on the form of a wolf. When the seven years are up, and if they have survived, two others take their place in the same way, and the first pair return to their

former country and nature. My companion in this pilgrimage is not far from here and is seriously ill. Please give her in her last hour the solace of the priesthood in bringing to her the revelation of the divine mercy'.

This is what he said, and the priest, full of fear, followed him as he went before him to a certain tree not far away. In the hollow of the tree, the priest saw a she-wolf groaning and grieving like a human being, even though her appearance was that of a beast. As soon as she saw him, she welcomed him in a human way, and then gave thanks also to God that in her last hour he had granted her such consolation. She then received from the hands of the priest all the last rites duly performed up to the last communion. This, too, she eagerly requested, and implored him to complete his good act by giving her the viaticum. The priest insisted that he did not have it with him, but the wolf, who in the meantime had gone a little distance away, came back again and pointed out to him a little wallet, containing a manual and some consecrated hosts, which the priest according to the custom of his country carried about with him, hanging from his neck, on his travels. He begged him not to deny to them in any way the gift and help of God, destined for their aid by divine providence. To remove all doubt, he pulled all the skin off the she-wolf from the head down to the navel, folding it back with his paw as if it were a hand. And immediately the shape of an old woman, clear to be seen, appeared. At that, the priest, more through terror than reason, communicated her as she had earnestly demanded, and she then devoutly received the sacrament. Afterwards, the skin which had been removed by the she-wolf resumed its former position. When all this had taken place – more in equity than with proper procedure – the wolf showed himself to them to be a man rather than a beast. He shared the fire with them during the whole of the night, and when morning came he led them over a great distance of the wood, and showed them the surest route on their journey. When they parted, he gave many thanks to the priest for the benefit he had conferred upon him, and promised to give him much more tangible evidence of his gratitude, if the Lord should call him back from the exile in which he was, and of which he had now completed two thirds.

The story finishes with an outline of a document recording the event that was sent to the pope in Rome, but contains no further information about these werewolves.[2] In a note on this story, it is highlighted that the Norse version tells of a whole race of Irishmen who opposed the teaching of St

4.2 Pictorial representation of the legend of a priest and werewolves (after MS Roy 13B. viii, thirteenth century).

Patrick and some of whose descendents were punished by being turned into wolves every seven years. A Bishop Patrick writes 'Certain men of Irish race have from their origin a strange nature'.[3] This refers to some

Irishmen as men-wolves. Other versions of this tale place it in Ossory. The
link to Ossory and wolves is possibly associated with one of the supposed
ancestors of the tribe, a man called Laighneach Wolflike.[4] It is said that the
curse was given by St Natalis, a disciple of St Patrick, and the founder and
abbot of Kilmanagh near Kilkenny.[5] Others say it was St Patrick himself
who cursed the people thus, after they refused to listen to him preach but
bayed at him like wolves. A manuscript version of *Topographia Hibernica*
by Giraldus Cambrensis contains variations on this story and states that it
occurred in 1182 in Co. Meath and that the priest was travelling from
Ulster. Each of the three parts of the story is illustrated with a simple line
drawing (fig. 4.2). The wolf-men of Ossory only attacked sheep and cattle
and not men, being true wolves in their nature. Werewolves of other
countries were considered to be devourers of human flesh. The wolf-men
were working out their saintly punishment and were not the evil
monstrous beings found in other countries. According to Cahill,

> The wolf transformations in Ireland have much more in common
> with the animal transformation practised in many parts of the world
> when seeking knowledge not available in human form, than they
> have with the manifestations of evil more commonly associated with
> European werewolves.[6]

This transformation is discussed by Camden in his Tipperary section, but
he calls this story 'fabulous', and states that it has to do with the disease of
lycanthropy and is not a true transformation, even if it is a transformation
in the mind of the individual concerned. He attributes this disease to
melancholy.[7] Lycanthropy is one of three medical conditions that could
easily have influenced medieval and earlier people to believe in werewolves. Clinical lycanthropy is a psychiatric condition in which an
individual believes that he or she has been transformed into an animal
such as a dog or a wolf.[8] The affected person develops a taste for raw meat
and has mannerisms that can include howling and running around naked.[9]
Given the primitive medical knowledge of the Middle Ages and earlier, it
is not surprising that the concept of werewolves could develop. This idea
of lycanthropy is mentioned by Giraldus Cambrensis.[10]

The next and most common is lupus erythematosus, of which one of
the main symptoms is sensitivity to light and, in extreme cases, the
shunning of all daylight.[11] The final and rarest medical condition, but also
the most dramatic, is hypertrichosis.[12] The hairiness of individuals varies
considerably and very hairy people were viewed with suspicion as being
potentially werewolves. However, hypertrichosis (also known as the

4.3 Petrus Gonzales (1648), the first recorded case of hypertrichosis (anonymous German depiction).

werewolf syndrome) in some cases involves extreme hair growth all over the body; so much so that the individuals affected take on a distinct animal appearance. Sufferers could be mistaken for werewolves and persecuted as a result. In more recent times, sufferers, including the bearded lady, worked in freak shows (if they ever appeared in public at all). Petrus

Gonzales from the Canary Islands suffered from hypertrichosis in the seventeenth century (fig. 4.3). Two of his daughters, one son and one grand-child also had the condition. The family were given the name the Ambras family and the condition became known as the Ambras Syndrome.

In 1596, Edmund Spenser, the poet and colonial administrator, had his dialogist Irenius recall the report that the Irish, like the Scythians, turn into wolves once a year.[13]

One of the big fears in medieval Europe was the relative invulnerability of werewolves, which could only be killed by a silver bullet (ideally blessed by a priest) or, more simply, by calling out three times the Christian name of the person who has been transformed. However, there is a possible rational explanation for the belief in werewolves and that was people affected by lycanthropy, as discussed above.

Another characteristic of humans that identified them as being a werewolf was eyebrows that met across the nose and this was generally considered to be a bad sign, perhaps because of the dark and frowning look they gave to the face and their association with a brooding or violent temper. This characteristic was used to denote an unlucky person in England, while in Scotland it was associated with early death, being unlucky in love, being an immoral person or being predestined to hang. In Greece it was linked with vampires, and werewolves in Denmark, Germany and Iceland.[14] Powerful shamans or holy men in many cultures used the spirit of the wolf as part of their power and ritual and were in some cases able to assume wolf form.[15]

Given this pan-European tradition of werewolves, it not surprising that this superstition can be found in Ireland also. However, there is a much wider and older pan-European superstition that humans in certain circumstances could change into wolves, and these people included wizards.[16] In Irish mythology, the cave of Owenagat, Co. Roscommon, was entrance to the otherworld (also known as the Irish entrance to Hell). Legend states that three female werewolves emerge from here every year and kill sheep; they are slain by *Caílte* and are described as the three daughters of *Airitech*, of the last of the Grevious Company from the Cave of Cruachua, and they prefer to rob in the shape of wolves rather than in human form.[17] Other examples include the Morrigan, who was said to have taken the form of a wolf with red fur in her battle with *Cú Cuchalainn*.[18]

Certain families in Ireland and in Scotland were traditionally said to be descended from foxes, wolves or seals.[19] A much more politically motivated view of the Irish being wolf-like was promoted by English political satirists in an attempt to demonize the Irish and justify their maltreatment. The earliest evidence of this is a record that there were a number of tailed (wolf) Irish among the slaughtered Irish garrison in Cashel, Co. Tipperary, in 1647. This was according to a captain of General Ireton's regiment who was present at the battle.[20] This view was enhanced using the ideas of naturalists of the eighteenth century, who were interested in so-called monstrous men of the woods, who were hybrids and therefore demonic in origin. This was transferred from the Jacobites to the Irish after the rebellions of 1798 and 1803. The Phoenix Park murders of 1882 were further used to justify ideas of the Irish as being sub-human and were compared to slaves turning on their masters. The representations of the simian Irish, the lupine Irish and the Irish man of the woods in Victorian caricatures further shows this politically motivated depiction.[21]

Trials in France in the sixteenth and seventeenth centuries of people accused of being werewolves led to hundreds of executions. Many of the victims were men, women and children with mental and physical disabilities. Even as late as 1927, a policeman near Strasbourg shot dead a boy he believed to be a werewolf and stood trial for the murder.[22]

Remarkably, the term *fear breagh* or wolf man is still in existence in the Slieve Blooms along the borders of Cos Laois and Offaly. This area had a long association with wolves. There are also two terms in Irish that are translated as werewolf; the modern word is *conriocht*, while the old Irish word *conoel* (*conaol*) refers to a female werewolf.[23] In the Brehon legal text *Bretha Crolige* (34), there is reference to a *confaol*, a female werewolf or a woman who strays abroad in the shape of a wolf.

CHAPTER 5

The historic record up to AD1786 and beyond?

INTRODUCTION

This chapter outlines the history of wolves in Ireland from the early medieval period up to 1786. Information on wolves is available in a wide variety of documents including the annals, Brehon Laws, government edicts and letters. The records include direct observations, attacks on livestock (rarely on humans), hunting of wolves by humans, bounties and bounty hunters and notices of the last wolves in various districts. At the end of the chapter, there is a brief discussion of the Irish wolf-dog, whose fame stretches all the way back to Roman times.

CHRONOLOGY OF RECORDED WOLF INCIDENTS

Wolves were so numerous in the woods and fastnesses of early medieval Ireland as to constitute a formidable danger to the community. In early Irish writings we meet with frequent notices of their ravages, and of the measures taken to guard against them.[1] Wolves were plentiful throughout the medieval period and they were tolerated, although hunted on occasion.[2] In his description of western and central Ireland around AD500, Young imagines it full of druids, monks and wolves.[3] The monk Augustine, writing in AD655, is credited with the mention of the first list of Irish species: wolf, red deer, wild boar, fox, badger, hare and squirrel.[4] With the addition of otter and seal, Augustine listed a total of nine species of mammal in Ireland, of which the wolf and wild boar have become extinct in this country.[5] Augustine, being familiar with the fauna of both Ireland and Britain, explained that wolves occurred naturally in Ireland and were not brought there by humans.[6]

In the eighth century, the monk Nennius described the wonders of Ireland. He claimed that, with the exception of the mouse, the wolf and the fox, Ireland did not currently or previously have any noxious animals.[7] Interestingly, there are no references in the written sources of the seventh and eighth centuries to the hunting of wolves by dogs, but wolves are listed among the three pet mammals taken from the wild – the other two were the fox and the deer.[8] An unidentified eighth-century book identifies wolves, foxes, deer and herons, which were kept as pets by the Irish.[9] The offences committed by the wolf were equated to those of the domestic dog, as all wild mammals were compared to their closest domestic equivalent (although in one version the Irish hare is equated to the domestic hen). In another Old Irish text, there is a short discussion of the legal implications when a domestic dog and a wolf (presumably a pet) together kill young sheep. The wolf was considered to be the principal predator of livestock, particularly lambs and calves. As a result, wolf-hunting was considered a public duty and, according to a ninth-century glossator on the law-text *Cáin Aicillne*, a client must hunt wolves once a week.[10]

There was a whole series of regulations governing human interaction with wolves from a farming perspective, and a list of herdsman's duties with respect to wolves.[11] It was illegal for a person to drive their neighbour's livestock into an area where a wolf pack was known to exist, and if he did so, he had to pay compensation for any animals that were killed. A herdsman tending livestock owned by another person was free from penalty for the first animal killed by a wolf, but not for any subsequent death. A different version relates that the herdsman was not liable for the first bite of the wolf, but was liable for all subsequent attacks, showing that he was as alert as could normally be expected in carrying out his duties. In addition, the herdsman was obliged to show the owner the carcass of the killed animal, demonstrating that he was quick enough to scare off the wolves before they had a chance to eat. These regulations also suggest that limited predation by wolves was an accepted part of the risks associated with rearing livestock and that small losses could be tolerated.

As early as AD962, there is a record of the Anglo-Saxon king, Edgar, imposing a tribute of three hundred dead wolves a year on a subject prince in Wales, at a time when much of the country was covered in forest.[12] A slightly different version of this states that

> At this time, England was dreadfully infested with wolves; in order to get rid of them, Edgar changed the tribute which the Welsh people used to pay to him in money, into 300 wolves' heads, to be paid every year; this expedient effectually cleared the country in three years of those rapacious animals and there have been no wolves in England since, excepting in collections of wild beasts brought from foreign parts.[13]

In the first written description of Ireland based on his visits in 1183 and 1185–6, Giraldus Cambrensis notes that wolves were ripe before their proper season and even whelp in the month of December.[14] As early as 1185, permission to hunt wolves in Ireland was being granted by the king of England. In a deed from *c*.1185, John, son of the king of England, granted Alard son of William various lands near Waterford as well as the hunting of stag, doe, pig, hare, rabbit and wolf.[15]

Wolves were also killed throughout Europe as a result of the Black Death.[16] Prior to 1360, the monk Ranulphus Higden, writing from Chester, notes in passing the presence of wolves in Ireland.[17] The murage charter of 1361 for Galway city lists the taxable goods in full and includes wolfskins, indicating that they were a common enough commodity.[18] The annals for 1420 state that many people were killed by wolves in that year, probably due to rabies.[19]

In the severe winters in the 1430s, wolves were active in many parts of Europe from Smolensk, Russia, in the east, to England in the west. In England, but not in Scotland or Ireland, this may have been the last time that wolves were reported.[20] In the winter of 1439, fourteen people were killed by wolves in Paris due to a deterioration in climate. With particularly wet summers and bitterly cold winters, the wolves became so hungry that they entered villages and towns, killing people for food.[21] This coincides with annalistic entries detailing increased frequencies of wolf attacks on human settlements in Ireland – it could be that depopulation from plague allowed wolves to expand their range.[22]

Bristol was the most important port for Irish exports, including wolfskins. The earliest reference to wolfskins from Ireland states that they were worth 1½*d*. in 1492. According to Ada Longfield, on 25 June 1505 the cargo list of a boat called the *Magdalen* of Waterford, captained by William Pembroke, included thirty-five wolfskins valued at 4*s*. 4*d*., with a subsidy of 2½*d*.[23] There is a possible reference to trade in wolfskins on 16 March 1517 for the *Mare Belhous* of Bristol, with John Harrys the master from Ireland. The entry is 0.5C skins, ouprars? valued at 8*s*. 4*d*., and the merchant's name is given as John Candell. There is no suggestion of what type of skin this was, hence the question mark.[24] It is noted that *pell'lupor* is used to indicate wolfskins in the volumes.[25] This is remarkably close to 'ouprars', given the language and un-standardized spelling used in the early 1500s. I suggest that these are most likely wolfskins. The vessel was also listed as carrying fox and otter skins as well as large quantities of sheep and salted skins. The 0.5C also presents some problems, as it could mean 56lbs (half a hundredweight) or sixty skins. If it were sixty skins, this would translate into just under 1½*d*. per skin, exactly the same as the value for 1504–5.[26]

A similar entry occurs on 9 June 1526 for the *Savior* of Wexford, with Robert Turnor the master. The master was the merchant listed for a dicker of 'skins? ouprar' valued at 2*s*. 6*d*. Again, it is suggested that ouprar here denotes wolf. A dicker is ten skins and this would value each skin at 3*d*., similar to previous wolfskin values.[27] The vessel was also carrying sheep, lamb and salted skins, the former two had much lower values per skin, whereas the salted skins (part-processed) had a higher value and it is suggested that this indicates that the raw ouprar was a high-value unprocessed skin.

There is no doubt about the remaining wolfskin entries outlined in table 5.1.[28] In all, thirty-eight definite wolfskins were imported into Bristol from Ireland, based on nine of the eleven customs books, with a possibility of more (as discussed above). The imports were both on Irish vessels, whose home port was Waterford (and one from New Ross) and English and Welsh vessels from Bristol and Milton Haven respectively. The custom book covering 1541–2 recorded eighteen wolfskins being imported from Ireland; the 1542–3 account recorded six; and the 1545–6 recorded twelve. The next custom book, for 1550–1, notes only two wolfskins and none of the last four custom books record any at all.[29] The value of

Table 5.1 Records of the import of wolfskins into Bristol from Ireland, based on eleven sample yearly custom books from 1503 to 1601 (after Flavin & Jones (2009); note: 1*s*. = 12*d*.).

Tax year	Date in Bristol	Vessel	Home port	Master	Merchant	No.	Value	Value per item
1541–2	13 May 1542	*Anthony*	Waterford	Henry Gall	Roland Harold	6	2*s*.	4*d*.
1541–2	13 May 1542	*Anthony*	Waterford	Henry Gall	Thomas Skyllan	5	20*d*.	4*d*.
1541–2	26 June 1542	*Sunday*	Bristol	Thomas Walter	Stephen Mewghe	3	2*s*. 6*d*.	10*d*.
1541–2	26 June 1542	*Sunday*	Bristol	Thomas Walter	David Richards	1	10*d*.	10*d*.
1541–2	26 June 1542	*Sunday*	Bristol	Thomas Walter	Richard White	1	10*d*.	10*d*.
1541–2	26 June 1542	*Sunday*	Bristol	Thomas Walter	Stephen White	2	20*d*.	10*d*.
1542–3	22 October 1542	*Bryde*	Waterford	Nicholas Cornycke	George Walter	2	8*d*.	4*d*.
1542–3	22 October 1542	*Bryde*	Waterford	Nicholas Cornycke	James Styrche	2	10*d*.	5*d*.
1542–3	28 January 1543	*Anthony*	Waterford	Henry Gall	Patrick Richards	2	8*d*.	4*d*.
1545–6	4 March 1546	*Andrew*	New Ross	Richard Doffe	Robert Leonard	3	2*s*.	8*d*.
1545–6	21 June 1546	*John*	Waterford	Richard Kyrry	George Brydgis	2	20*d*.	10*d*.
1545–6	15 July 1546	*Anthony*	Milford Haven	John Brother	Thomas Nayle	4	3*s*. 4*d*.	10*d*.
1545–6	21 July 1546	*Trynyte*	Waterford	Thomas Butler	Peter Creagh	2	20*d*.	10*d*.
1545–6	21 July 1546	*Trynyte*	Waterford	Thomas Butler	Thomas Ferrys	1	8*d*.	8*d*.
1550–1	25 July 1551	*Fawkon*	Waterford	Robert Medwell	Robert Walsh	2	20*d*.	10*d*.

wolfskins varied from 4*d*. to 10*d*., even in the same year, and this variation must be a reflection of the size and quality of the skin.

By 1553, the value of wolfskins had risen to 8*d*. each.[30] In 1558, a total of 731 wolfskins were landed from Ireland: 321 from Cork boats, 160 from Youghal boats, 149 from Waterford boats and 101 from Ross (Co. Cork) boats. They were valued at 8*d*. each, so the price had not changed since 1553. In the following tax year (1558–9), a remarkable total of 961 wolfskins were exported from Ireland to Bristol and these were valued at £32 1*s*. 4*d*. It is further noted that throughout the sixteenth and earlier centuries an average of between one hundred and three hundred wolfskins were exported from Ireland to Bristol each year. As discussed later (p. 81), however, there is some doubt about the accuracy of these figures.

In 1600, dense woods covered about 12.5 per cent of Ireland and among the animals they sheltered were wolves.[31] From about this time onwards, wolves were systematically persecuted,[32] but before that time they were generally tolerated, although hunted on occasion.[33] They seem to have become more plentiful in the sixteenth and seventeenth centuries.[34] When the English authorities converted an abbey church in Derry into a fort and magazine around 1567, a large and hairy wolf caused an explosion in it.[35] According to Edward Campion, 'they (the Irish) are not without wolves or greyhounds to hunt them; bigger of bone and limme than a colt'.[36] According to one commentator, writing *c*.1570,

> In Ireland as I have heard, there are a great store of them; and because many noblemen and gentlemen have a desire to bring that countrie to be inhabited and civilly governed (and would God there were more of the same kind), therefore I have thought good to set down the nature and manner of hunting the wolf according to mine author.[37]

According to F.A. Allen,

> An open spot was generally chosen at some distance from the great coverts where the wolves were known to lie, and here in concealment, a brace, or sometimes two brace, of wolfhounds were placed. A horse was killed, and the forequarters were trailed about as a lure. When night approached, out came the wolves, and having struck the scent they followed it and began to feed upon the flesh, and early in the morning, just before daybreak, the hunters placed the dogs so as to prevent the wolves from returning to cover. When a wolf came to the spot, the men in charge suffered him to pass by the first dogs; but the last were let slip at him, and so he was surrounded and killed.[38]

1 A pack of grey wolves at Dublin Zoo, 2011 (photograph courtesy of Gary Wilson).

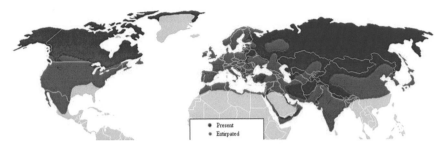

2 Past and present distribution of the grey wolf (*Canis lupus*).

3 Wolves communicate to each other and protect their territory by howling. They don't bark like domestic dogs and nor do they howl at the moon. But on a clear night when the moon is clear the sound travels much further (photograph courtesy of Gary Wilson).

4 Image from a thirteenth-century bestiary showing a wolf approaching a sheep-pen as the shepherd sleeps (reproduced by kind permission of the Fitzwilliam Museum, Cambridge).

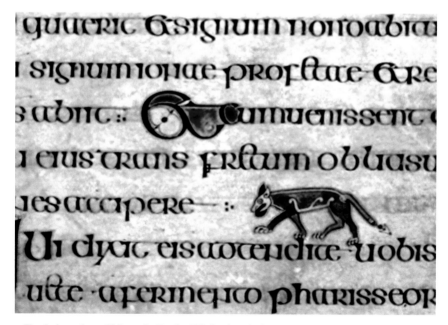

5 Depiction of a wolf from the Book of Kells, fo. 76v (reproduced by kind permission of the Board of Trinity College, Dublin).

6 The urban hyena in Africa. Do we want people wandering our street with 'pet' wolves or wolf cross hybrids?

7 A wolf chorus (photograph courtesy of Gary Wilson).

8 Wolves will eat virtually anything but prefer large mammals such as deer (photograph courtesy of Gary Wilson).

9 Grey wolves at Dublin Zoo, 2011 (photograph courtesy of Gary Wilson).

10 Group bonding; one of the core reasons why wolf packs are so formidable
(photograph courtesy of Gary Wilson).

11 Wolves at rest (photograph courtesy of Gary Wilson).

12 The powerful jaws of a wolf (photograph courtesy of Gary Wilson).

13 Wolves resting; content but vigilant (photograph courtesy of Gary Wilson).

A variation of this account says that a horse was killed and divided in two.[39] The fore-part was trailed through a wood and dragged to a clearing with the hind-part (which was not trailed, to prevent the scatter of viscera); the wolves came to feed at night and were easily ambushed. There is some doubt about this hunting method, as it would depend on keeping the dogs quiet and remaining downwind of the wolf.[40] These descriptions give some insight into wolf behaviour. They were nocturnal and took carrion and they generally resided in deep cover or possibly even caves.

The native forests of Ireland were seen as such an obstacle to the Elizabethan armies in Ireland in the 1580s that many schemes were thought up to get rid of them. It was also believed that they were the haunt of rebels (known as woodkerne) and wolves.[41] As the population and the extent of open cultivated land increased, wolves became less numerous, but during the wars of the reign of Elizabeth, when the country was greatly depopulated, wolf numbers increased enormously and they became bolder and fiercer, so that we often find notices of their attacks in the literature of those times.[42] In 1584, wolves committed great ravages among the flocks in the south-west of the country:[43]

> and whosoever did travell from the one end unto the other of all Munster, he should not meet anie man, woman or child, saving in townes and cities, not yet see anie beast, but the verie wolves, the foxes and other like ravening beasts; many of them laie dead, being famished, and the residue gone elsewhere.[44]

As a result of the wreck of three Spanish Armada vessels on 25 September 1588 off Streedagh Strand, Co. Sligo, more than six hundred corpses were cast up by the sea and were left to be devoured by ravens and wolves.[45] This information comes from a letter written by Francisco de Cuellar, who was on board the galleon *San Pedro* and was one of the surviving officers who wrote an account of the events.

After the destruction in 1591 of Kilmallock, Co. Limerick, by James Fitzmaurice, it was stated to have been the haunt of wolves.[46] Lord William Russell, lord deputy of Ireland, recorded in his diary that on 26 May 1596 he and Lady Russell went wolf hunting at Kilmainham, close to the city of Dublin.[47]

Prior to 1596, Edmund Spenser, in his incomplete epic poem *The Fairie Queen*, was inspired by the landscape of Munster with the background of forest and ravine, haunted by outlaws and wolves.[48] After the Battle of the Yellow Ford in 1598, the duke of Ormond made the comment that it was madness to use poorly trained conscripts and expect them to defeat a foe as tireless and savage as the wolves still lurking in the forests of Ireland. This is one of the many comparisons made between the native Irish rebels and wolves. The great earl of Tyrone, on meeting Queen Elizabeth's grandson, John Harington, in Ireland in 1599, began by describing his own hard life, comparing himself to wolves that fill their bellies sometimes and go without food at other times.[49]

Cattle and livestock generally were liable to be carried off by thieves or attacked by dogs and wolves.[50] Peter Lombard, primate of Ireland, noted that large Irish hunting dogs were employed for capturing stags, boars and wolves.[51] Fynes Moryson, in his description of Ulster after the Elizabethan Wars in 1600–1, remarked on the almost complete devastation of many parts of the province and that wolves pulled down grown men in broad daylight.[52] Moryson, who was secretary to lord deputy Mountjoy between 1599 and 1603, went on to note that

> for fear of thieves (the Irish using no other kind of theft), or else for fear of wolves, the destruction whereof being neglected by the inhabitants, oppressed with greater mischiefs, they are so much grown in numbers as sometimes on winter nights they will come and prey in villages and suburbs of cities … The cattle had to be driven in at night for fear of thieves or else for fear of wolves.[53]

After the Battle of Kinsale in 1601, the hungry wolves sallied forth to attack men weak with hunger. According to O'Sullivan Beare, the wolves came 'out of the wood and mountains, attacked and tore to pieces the people enfeebled by want of food'.[54] Not long later, in reference to Bandon, Co. Cork, Richard Boyle, the earl of Cork, stated that

> The place where Bandon Bridge is situated, upon a great district of the country, was within the last twenty-four years a mere waste bog and wood serving as a retreat and harbour to woodkernes, rebels, thieves and wolves and yet now (God be praised) as civil a plantation as most in England.[55]

A letter from Sir Arthur Chichester to Sir John Davys in 1609 included a section dealing with the plantation of Ulster:

> If the Irish do not possess and inhabit a great part of the lands in some of those escheated counties, none but wolves and wild beasts would possess them for many years to come; for where civil men may have lands for reasonable rents in so many thousand places in that

province, and in this whole kingdom, they will not plant themselves in mountains, rocks and desert places, though they might have the land for nothing.[56]

As a major period of deforestation of the remaining oak forests began after *c*.1609, wolves were increasingly confined to smaller and smaller patches of secondary woodland.[57] During the early phases of the various plantations, precautions were taken against threats to the settlers. The most serious threats, according to Lord Blennerhassett in 1610, were posed by wolves and woodkerne, who were bracketed together and inhabited similar ground. Blennerhassett goes on to say that periodic manhunts should be conducted to hunt down the human wolves in their lairs.[58] It is eye-opening to see the line between wolves and Irish rebels being blurred to indistinction. The wolf metaphor is used throughout to describe humans, in a propaganda tool designed to heighten loathing of the Irish rebels. Blennerhassett went on to note that

> Sir Toby Caulfield's people (in the county of Armagh) are driven every night to lay up all his cattle, as it were inward, and do he and his what they can, the wolfe and the wood-kerne, within culiver shot of his fort, and oftentimes a share.[59]

A small group of letters among the Carew Manuscripts in London give an insight into the activities of the seignory of Kinalmeaky, Co. Cork, under Sir Bernard Greville, and one letter of 1611 notes that Roger Braben is mainly concerned with the growth of his stud of horses but also states that a colt had been killed by a wolf.[60]

In the reign of James I in 1611, an act was passed for the killing of wolves and other vermin.[61] In spite of the act, it was considered necessary to kill more wolves than just for sporting purposes, as they remained a menace to both livestock and people.[62] Both the wolf and the wild boar were said to have disappeared during the reign of Charles II (1660–85),[63] but this relates to England, Wales and Scotland and not Ireland.

In the first year of the reign of Queen Anne, as the colonization of the territory of the O'Dempseys was occurring, the wolf (among other creatures) was in retreat, the only evidence of their presence being in occasional place-names.[64] According to Thomas Gainsford's *Glory of England*, written in 1619, the wolves forced the population of Ulster to 'house their cattle in the bawnes of their castles, where all the winter nights they stood up to their bellies in dirt'.[65] The smell must have been particularly awful and provided an added incentive for the settlers to get rid of the woods, wolves and woodkerne.

After the wars of 1641, wolf numbers increased to such an extent, and their ravages became so great, that wolf-hunters were appointed in various parts of Ireland.[66] There is no clear indication of the cause of this increase, but it is likely to have been due to the devastation and mass slaughter and famine associated with the Cromwellian Wars. Although the wolf does not normally eat carrion, the huge numbers of unburied bodies after the 1641 rising resulted in a great increase in available food.[67] Wolves have been known to exhume bodies at times of shortage of other sources of food. *Ireland's tragical tyrannie* (1642), a politically motivated tract, tells the story of a family of fourteen called Adams who, during the rebellion, fled into the woods and were all devoured by wolves.[68]

In what can only be described as a piece of the most bizarre and perverse logic, Cromwell in 1650 stated that

> For if the priests had not been in Ireland, the trouble would not have arisen, nor the English have come, nor have made the country almost a ruinous heap, nor would the wolves have so increased.[69]

Ireland was long celebrated for her wolf-dogs, which were considered fit presents for kings.[70] In 1652, officers leaving for Spain, proud of their dogs, were found to be taking them with them. According to Harting, customs officers at the different ports, now crowded with these departing exiles, were directed to seize the dogs, on account of the increasing number of the wolves, and send them to the public huntsman of the precinct.[71] The 'Declaration against the transporting of wolfe dogges' reads as follows:

> Forasmuch as we are credibly informed, that wolves doe much increase and destroy many cattle in several partes of this dominion, and that some of the enemie's party, who have laid down armes, and have liberty to go beyond the sea, and others, do attempt to carry away such great dogges as are commonly called wolfe dogges, whereby the breed of them, which are useful for the destroying of wolves, would (if not prevented) speedily decay. These are, therefore, to prohibit all persons whatsoever from exporting any of the said dogges out of this dominion; and searchers and other officers of the customs, in the several partes and creekes of this dominion, are hereby strictly required to seize and make stopp of all such dogges, and deliver them either to the common huntsman, appointed for the

precinct where they are seized upon, or to the governor of the said precinct. Dated at Kilkenny, 27 April 1652 – Council Book A.[72]

At the same time, rewards were offered of £5 and £6 respectively for male and female wolves.[73] A reward of £2 was given for a hunting cub and 10s. for a suckling cub. This very lucrative set of bounties had the desired effect with a rapid reduction in wolf numbers.[74] Commonwealth passes were even given to certain Irishmen who were trusted to hunt wolves:

> Ordered that Richard Toole, with Morris McWilliam, his servant, with their two fowling pieces, and half a pound of powder and bullet proportionable be permitted to pass quietly from Dublin into the counties of Kildare, Wicklow and Dublin, for the killing of wolves. To continue for the space of two months from the date of the order. Dublin, 1 November 1652.[75]

Public hunts were regularly organized and deer toils (traps/snares) were brought over from England and kept in the public store for setting up while 'driving the woods with hounds and horn for these destructive beasts of prey'.[76] On 20 December 1652, measures were taken for the destruction of wolves in the barony of Castleknock, Co. Dublin.[77] This occurred in the Scaldwood, some six miles from Dublin.[78]

War conditions, of course, had been favourable to the continued existence of the wolf.[79] Although much reduced by the deforestation of the country, at the end of the Cromwellian campaigns (1649–53) these animals were so numerous up to the outskirts of Dublin that a regular pack of wolfhounds was established in Co. Meath under the terms of a lease of 1653.[80]

Wolves are referred to in another document produced by Cromwell's council, the 'Declaration touching the poor':

> Upon serious consideration had of the great multitude of poor, swarming in all parts of this nation, occasioned by the devastations of the country, and the habit of licentiousness and idleness which the generality of the people have acquired in the time of this rebellion, insomuch, that some are found feeding on carrion and weeds, some starved in the highways, and many times poor children, who lost their parents, or deserted by them, are found exposed to, some of them fed upon by ravenous wolves, and other beasts and birds of prey; the said commissioners conceive it a duty incumbent upon them, to use all honest and laudable ways and means for the relief of such poor people. Dated at Dublin, 12 May 1653 – Council Book.[81]

On 29 June 1653, district commissioners were ordered to appoint days for hunting wolves under bounty, and this order was reissued on 1 July 1656:[82]

> By a printed declaration of 29 June 1653, republished on 1 July 1656, the commanders of the various districts were to appoint days and times for hunting the wolf; and persons destroying wolves and bringing their heads to the commissioners of the revenue of the precinct were to receive for the head of a bitch wolf, £6; of a dog wolf, £5; for the head of every cub that preyed by himself, 40s.; for the head of every suckling cub 10s. Book of the Declarations of the Commissioners for the Affairs of Ireland'.[83]

One wonders how it was possible to tell the head of an adult male wolf from that an adult female. The difference of £1 would have been quite a sum at the time, and the temptation must have been to say that the adult wolf heads were all female. The assessments on several counties to reimburse the treasury for those advances became a serious charge.[84] In December 1665, the inhabitants of Co. Mayo petitioned the council of state, stating that the commissioners of assessment might be at liberty to compound for wolf-heads.[85] The 'Declaration touching wolves' states that

> For the better destroying of wolves, which of late years have much increased in most parts of this nation, it is ordered that the commanders in chiefe and commissioners of the revenue in the several precincts, doe consider of, use and execute all good wayes and meanes, how the wolves, in the counties and places within the respective precincts, may be taken and destroyed; to employ such person or persons, and to appoint such daies and tymes for hunting the wolfe, as they shall adjudge necessary. And it is further ordered, that all such person or persons as shall take, kill, or destroy any wolfes, and shall bring forth the head of the woulfe before the said commanders of the revenue, shall receive the sums following, viz., for every bitch wolf, six pounds; for every dogg wolfe, five pounds; for every cubb which prayeth for himself, forty shillings; for every suckling cubb, ten shillings; And no woolfe after the last of September until 10 January be accounted a young woolfe, and the commissioners of the revenue shall cause the same to equallie assessed within their precincts. Dated at Dublin 29 June 1653.[86]

In the time of Cromwell, parts of Ireland continued to be much infested by wolves.[87] As a result of the desolation caused by the Cromwellian Wars, there was an almost complete breakdown of food production and a disintegration of Irish families, particularly the separation of men from women and children. As a result, some children who had lost their parents were attacked and eaten by wolves. Wandering orphans whose fathers went to join the army in Spain and whose mothers had died of famine were preyed upon by wolves.[88] The wolves were also a cause of trouble to the adventurers and soldiers, who had driven the Irish over the Shannon, and wolf hunts were regularly organized. D'Alton notes that the Tories were even worse than the wolves, and describes Tories or Idle Boys living in organised bands and falling like wolves on the English settlers.[89]

By 1653, even Inishbofin off the coast of Connemara had been taken by the Cromwellians and famine and pestilence stalked the land.[90] Starvation was widespread, with wolves coming right into the towns and carrying off people from outlying houses. It is stated in the 'terrier' attached to the Down Survey map (1655–6) of Ballybay, Co. Offaly, that few sheep were kept in that barony on account of the prevalence of wolves there.[91]

At the first meeting of the united parliament of the three kingdoms on 10 June 1657 (1659?), a Major Morgan, MP for Wicklow, proclaimed that

> We have three beasts to destroy that lay burthensome upon us. The first is the wolf, on whom we lay five pounds a head if a dog, and ten pounds if a bitch; the second beast is a priest, on whose head we lay ten pounds, and if he is eminent more. The third beast is the Tory and on his head, if he be a public Tory, we lay ten pounds, and if he is a private Tory, we pay 40 shillings.[92]

The association between wolves and outlaws was common in Europe, as both were seen as outside the law and could be killed with impunity. In England, a condemned person was made to wear a wolf's head mask and even the gibbets were named 'wolf's head tree' during the eleventh century.[93] The association between outlaws and wolves helped to generate the idea of a werewolf in the popular imagination.

What follows is a series of excerpts relating to wolves from letters in the State Papers for the 1650s and 1660s. The letters are addressed to Viscount Conway from his agent, Sir George Rawdon. The 'Collen' referred to is Collin Mountain and 'Tunny Park' is the district along the edge of Lough Neagh between Glenavy and Portmore.[94]

> Dublin 26 May 1657
> I am not sure yet of finding the Ayry: yet a probability the wolves did so haunt and undo the tenants in those islands by the loughside that

their noise, hunting and horning, were very like to have skarred the hawks.

Moyra 11 July 1657
I have at length got a good portion of moss and this morning had them put in a box (the skulls or part of them with it) and sent it on Monday to find the first passage to Chester; also the dogs which it is a pity to send out of the country, especially one of them. They have been about The Collen and above Mr Doynes this six weeks, and had some courses at wolves which exceedingly infest this country.

Dublin 9 December 1657
I have your lordship's two wolf-dogs … I have two more that bare kept to hunt the wolf upon every occasion he commits spoil; then the people come still to borrow them out.[95]

Lisburn 3 September 1665
The wolf haunts the park (Tunny) of late and hath killed 3 or 4 of a few muttons … so I have put Totall upon setting traps and watching with guns, and Simon the keeper, who is an excellent shot, but I perceive no great woodman, yet I hope will do well being careful and not given to drink.[96]

Lisburn 7 October 1665
The keepers and all our gun men are watching the wolves that haunt the Tunny Park almost every night.[97]

It is clear that wolves continued to be very troublesome, as the Commonwealth record for 29 August 1659 notes that

Whereas some money had been issued on account to Colonel Daniel Abbott and others, for providing of toyles for taking of wolves, which had been brought over for publique use; and understanding the part thereof is at present at Greenhill, near Kilcullen; ordered that Captain Tomlins, comptroller of ye traine, do forthwith take care of the said toyles and other materials thereto belonging be brought from Greenhill, or any other place, and laid in the publique store, and there kept until further direction shall be given concerning the same. Thos. Herbert, clerk of the council.[98]

Collin Mountain behind Belfast was infested with wolves in the 1660s, as was the eastern side of Lough Neagh. In the latter area, some leases that probably date from the early eighteenth century, bound tenants to kill a certain number of wolves during their tenancy.[99] In Revd G.N. Nuttall-Smith's *Chronicles of a Puritan family in Ireland*, the author affirms that at the close of the Civil War about the year 1660, wolves were still hunted in the neighbourhood of Dublin.[1] In the *Journal of the House of Commons* for 1662 there is notice of a report from Sir John Ponsonby from the committee of grievances that a bill should be brought in to encourage the killing of wolves and foxes.[2]

The following is an extract from a 1663 petition from William Collowe to the duke of Ormond, lord lieutenant of Ireland:

> That yor grace petr through God's assistance and his owne industry hath found a way for the destroying the ravenous wolfe and other vermin wch much annoy his maties subjects the poor inhabitants of his kingdome, and being desirous to imrove his tallent he is now lately arived in this kingdome and purposeth with God's assitants and yr graces comission to goe on upon the worke with all expedicion. May it therefore please yor grace to grant yor ordr to yr petr and his assistants to use all means and to have free egresse and regresse in all places in this kingdome for the doing of the worke above mencioned. And allsoe that all justices of the peace, majors, sheriffs and other officers may be required to punish and restrain all persons, or any person, that shall use the same way with yor grace supld, until he hath perfected his worke in killing the wolves of this kingdome (his way being more than ordinary, and never knowne in this kingdome, allthough it may be with much difficulty attained and stollen from yor petr he having once layd the groundworke) except as shall be deputated by him, and allsoe that justices within this kingdome shall order such sattisfacon to be given yor graces petr for each wolfe destroyed by him and his as in yor graces wisdome shall think fitt: all which he submitts to yor grace and desists. Yor Graces dayly Orator Will Collowe.[3]

In 1663, Christopher Croaffts, in Co. Down, wrote to Sir John Perceval that 'we are much troubled with wolves for we lost at Wailshistowne three sheep; another night at Ballyadam four sheep.'[4]

In 1669, Grand Duke Cosimo III de' Medici, writing about his travels in England, referred to wolves as being common in Ireland and mentions that mastiffs were in great demand for hunting them.[5] Similarly, Brodin in the same year noted that large greyhounds were kept in Ireland for the hunting of wolves.[6] As late as 1673, wolves were still sufficiently plentiful to be regarded as common in Co. Cork, according to a letter from Lord Broghill, who was living in Charleville at the time. The letter was sent to the earl of Dorset. Broghill even had a tame wolf, presumably one caught as a cub and reared by humans.[7] An entry dated 22 April 1676 in the Youghal Corporation Council Book notes that £3 15s. 4d. was charged on the town and liberties of Youghal, by order of the late justices of assize, towards the taking of wolves and foxes, to be paid by the mayor out of the town revenue.[8]

Around 1672, it was noted that in the more remote county of Leitrim, the wolves which had been very numerous were now few, thanks to the care of the justices at the quarter sessions who paid a bounty of 2d. per hearth out of every hearth in the barony where the service was done.[9] The notes were prepared by Teague O'Roddy. They were sent to Thomas Molyneaux to be included in an atlas by Moses Pitt.

In 1677 it was stated that 'they have routes (that is, hunting) of wolves to this very day in Ireland'.[10] In a manuscript of 1683 it was stated that the wolf-dog and the wolf were two quadrupeds present in Ireland but not in England.[11] Writing about west Connaught in 1684, O'Flaherty noted that the land there produced wild beasts such as wolves, but they were not as numerous as in the early part of the seventeenth century.[12] John Dunton on his travels through Ireland wrote of the impact of wolves in Connaught in the latter half of the seventeenth century:

> I had but just compos'd my selfe to sleep when I was strangely sur-
> prised to heare the cows and sheep all comeing into my bed chamber.
> I enquired the meaneing and was told it was to preserve them from
> the wolfe which everie night was rambling about for prey.[13]

Cromwell's official wolf-hunters were succeeded by a sort of professional class who made a living out of the sport.[14] In the 1690s in Co. Tyrone, where wolves were a great plague and even raided the stone enclosures made to protect sheep, a professional wolf-hunter named Rory Carragh was offered a substantial reward to kill two particular wolves which had escaped extermination. Carragh undertook the task with a little boy, the only person he could get to accompany him. He told the boy to attend to the dog's warning and not to fall asleep. As the night was very dark and cold, the boy started to get sleepy. Suddenly, the dog leapt across him with a roar and levelled the wolf. The boy bravely drove a spear through the wolf's neck and at that moment Carragh appeared at the entrance with the head of the other wolf.

Another story from Co. Tyrone relates that the final wolf was killed by a horse in defence of her foal.[15] In a book on the British Isles published in Nuremberg, Germany, in 1690, the wilds of Co. Kerry were referred to as a haunt of wolves.[16] In 1691, Echard wrote that the wild Irish prayed for wolves and wished them well, so that the people were not afraid to be hurt by them, as Ireland was much troubled with wolves.[17] Compton, writing in 1823, claimed that 'the last wolf seen in Ireland [was] killed with wolf-dogs on the hill of Aughnabrack, near Belfast, by Clotworthy Upton of Castle-Upton, Templepatrick.'[18] This date (1823) is clearly too late by a good margin. There is a further claim that the last wolf was killed at Nappan Mountain, Co. Antrim, in 1712.[19] A similar claim notes that the last wolf was killed near Lough Carra in Co. Mayo, but it is not clear if this was just the last wolf in this area.[20] In the Barrett–Lennard papers there is reference to fourteen wolves inhabiting Slieve Beagh in north Monaghan in November 1696. In a letter dated to 1698, an alderman in Cork by the name of Howel states that wolves were still present in his locality, but that they were now considered as game and diversion as opposed to noxious and hateful.[21] This indicates that their numbers were in significant decline in this area. Also in 1698, in a return of the stock of William Conyngham in Co. Down, it was recorded that a two-year-old from his stock of black cattle had been killed by a wolf, without any indication that the incident was particularly remarkable.[22]

Bishop Downes noted that Mount Gabriel (Schull) and Berehaven in Co. Cork were still the haunt of wolves in 1699.[23] There is no doubt that by 1700 there were a number of packs of hunting hounds kept privately for the hunting of wolves, particularly in the counties of Kildare, Wicklow, Cork and Waterford.[24] Another wolf was killed at Warringstown, Co. Down, beside the old mill in the centre of the village in 1699 or 1700.[25]

As recently as the late seventeenth century, Ireland was also known as 'Wolfland'.[26] This is a clear indication of the numbers of wolves to be found at this time. By the end of the seventeenth century, the old forests were no more but the wolves were not yet extinct and cattle and other livestock were liable to be attacked by wolves. Bishop Dive Downes noted in his diary the presence of wolves and eagles in the Berehaven area or West Cork during his visit in June 1700 without any particular excitement.[27]

In his great statistical account of Scotland, Sinclair claims the last wolf was killed in Ireland in 1709.[28] According to Joyce, the last wolf in Ireland was killed *c.*1730.[29] The remarkable number of claims for last wolves in various counties between 1700 and 1712 indicates a period of significant fragmentation and decline in the Irish wolf population. One account notes that the last wolf in Joyce Country, west of Lough Mask, was killed in 1700.[30] The last wolf in Co. Laois was killed at Wolfhill in 1700 and the lords justices granted John Boate a reward for killing it.[31] The last wolf in Connaught was killed around 1700, and in Kerry around 1710.[32] Smith, writing in 1756 and much closer to the events he described, stated that certain ancient enclosures had been built to secure cattle from wolves, and that the latter were not finally killed off until about 1710.[33] The evidence to support this comprised presentments for raising money to destroy them, as recorded in some old grand-jury books. However, in a footnote in these books, a date of 1720 for the last wolf in Co. Kerry is mentioned.[34] More recently, a date of 1700 has been suggested for the final kill of a Kerry wolf in the MacGillycuddy's Reeks.[35]

It has been suggested that the last wolf in Glendalough, Co. Wicklow, was killed in 1700 or 1710.[36] A young wolf was taken alive from Collatin, Co. Wicklow, on 28 October 1713 by Dennis Duiggen, however, and was presented to Thomas Watson-Wentworth, who owned a very large estate in the Wicklow Mountains, where the wolf was probably caught. Many parts of these mountains at this time were wild and desolate.[37] The capture of a young wolf indicates that they were still breeding in Wicklow at this time. Elsewhere, it is noted that a wolf was shot in 1700 in Glenshane, Co. Derry, by Cormac O'Neill.[38] There is a further claim that another wolf was killed in Co. Derry at Tamlaght O'Crilly parish at a site called Wolf's Hill, while a man told an official that his grandfather had killed the last wolf in the woods of Ballyscullion, also in Co. Derry.[39] Wolves were so rapidly disappearing that in the early part of the eighteenth century the appearance of a wolf was considered something of a rarity in the counties of Galway and Mayo.[40]

In 1710, a last presentment was made to the grand jury in Co. Cork for killing wolves.[41] This date is also mentioned for the last kill of a wolf at Kilcrea, Co. Cork. The hunter was identified as Brian Townsend.[42] Elsewhere it is stated that the last wolf recorded in Co. Cork was killed in 1714.[43] A man used to point out to his son a spot up in the hills halfway between the sea at Ballycotton Bay and Fermoy where local tradition indicated that the last wolf was killed. No date or historical source is given but it is suggested that it was in the 1700s.[44] A poem of 1719 entitled

'McDermott, or the Irish fortune hunter' suggests that wolf-killing was a popular sport in Munster at that time.[45]

A letter from William Butler, high sheriff of Co. Clare, to secretary Dawson at Dublin Castle, dated Ennis 13 May 1712, states that

> Sir Donough O'Brien brigadier general, and Mr Thomas Hickman joyne their diligence with myne but I believe it would be easier at this time to ketch soe manye wolfes or foxes than those priests, their being twelve presented as mentioned in my laste for saying mass contrary to the statute.[46]

In 1877, a Mr Jonathan Grubb of Sudbury wrote to Mr Harting to relate some wolf stories from his family's history in Ireland:[47]

> I am now in my seventieth year. My father, who was born in 1767, used to tell wolf stories to us when we were children. His mother related them to him. Her maiden name was Malone; and her uncles were the actors in the scenes described at Ballyroggin, Co. Kildare. She remembered one of them, James Malone, telling her how his brother came home one night on horseback pursued by a pack of wolves, who overtook him and continued leaping on the hind quarters of his horse till he reached his own door, crying out 'Oh! James, James my horse is ate with the wolves'.[48]

The precise date of this story cannot be ascertained, but it suggests that wolves existed in Co. Kildare in the first quarter of the eighteenth century. A date of 1766 is sometimes suggested for the last wolf in Kildare.[49] According to H.D. Richardson, he was acquainted with an old gentleman between 80 and 90 years of age, whose mother remembered wolves being killed in Co. Wexford about 1730–40.[50] In 1707, Miege stated that 'wolves still abound too much in Ireland',[51] but Hardiman, writing in 1820, dismisses the likelihood of wolves still existing in Ireland at this time.[52] Lamb, erroneously in Ireland's case, states that the last wolves were seen and shot in Scotland and Ireland around 1740.[53] According to letters in the Lodge Collection in Armagh, it is suggested that the wolves had disappeared from this county at least some years before 1745.[54]

Lord Chesterfield, writing in 1750, stated that 'I have been trying these two years to get some of those large dogs of Ireland; but the breed has grown extremely rare there by the extinction of their enemies, the wolves'.[55] This ties in roughly with a letter from the bishop of Derry, which outlines when the last wolf was killed in Ireland:

The story I heard from Mr Duncan, who had a little hotel at Dungiven, was told to me by him when I was a very little boy, probably about 1834. Mr Duncan seemed to me then the oldest man that ever wore grey hair. I daresay he was over 80. Supposing that he was when the wolf was executed on the hill above Pollipar, about my age in 1834 as he said, that would take us to something between 1750 or 1760. Many years ago in an annual register of 1760 I read of the killing of a wolf in Ireland. Although Mr Duncan told me the wolf story so long ago it is thoroughly engraved in my memory.[56]

Another account gives a date of *c*.1763 for this event and explains that the wolf was discovered at Benevenagh and was hunted into the woods near Dungiven, where it was slain.[57] The tradition of 'the last wolf in Ireland' was particularly strong in two other nearby locations: Cluntygeragh and Craigashoke near Draperstown.[58] Wolves lingered in Glenconkeyne, Co. Derry, until the 1760s.[59] An edition of the works of James Ware covering the period 1739–64 indicates that there were no wolves in Ireland at that time.[60]

As the eighteenth century progressed, wolves were cleared from county after county, so that they were present in small numbers in only few locations – such as in Co. Kerry – which still had pockets of forest.[61] The general consensus is that the wolf became extinct in Ireland by about 1770, although later dates are also indicated.[62] Several sources suggest that the last wolf was killed in the Wicklow Mountains at this time.[63] It is interesting to note that Rutty makes no mention of wolves in his 1772 *Natural history of County Dublin*,[64] while in 1787 Lewis noted that wolf-dogs had become very scarce because of the extermination of wolves.[65] Elsewhere, it is claimed that the last wolf was killed in the Knockmealdown Mountains between Tipperary and Waterford, *c*.1770,[66] while other commentators give the location as Wolfhill, near Belfast.[67] Among the later dates suggested for the death of Ireland's last wolf are 1776,[68] 1782[69] and 1786. It is said in some quarters that the last wolf was exterminated in Co. Carlow in 1786 by the wolf-hounds of John Watson, master of the hounds at Myshall, near Ballydarton.[70] It is not clear where exactly this wolf was caught, but it may have been at Baltinglass, Co. Wicklow,[71] or on Mount Leinster on the Carlow/Wexford border, where Watson's daughter claimed the wolf had been killing sheep, and met its end on the banks of a stream.[72]

It may never be possible to prove categorically exactly when and where the last wolf was killed but somewhere between 1770 and 1786 is most likely, based on present evidence.

DISCUSSION AND ANALYSIS OF RECORDED INCIDENTS

This section is an analysis of the above documentary records of wolves in all their different types. Of course, there is no way of knowing how representative the surviving records of wolves are in terms of their temporal and spatial distribution, although enough records have survived in order to at least make some initial observations.

There are 129 documentary records of wolves in the above chronology from AD500 to 1786. All barring a handful occur in the sixteenth, seventeenth and eighteenth centuries (fig. 5.1). Most records occur in the seventeenth century and this reflects the plantations of Ulster and Munster, the associated Cromwellian and Williamite Wars and the growing use of English as the language of record. It also reflects the horror of the colonists on arriving in Ireland to find that wolves were common across the country. The second highest total comes from the eighteenth century and this is a result of the huge numbers of notices of last wolves at various scales from local to national.

A more detailed assessment is carried out using the decadal numbers from 1490 to 1790 (fig. 5.2). This shows an initial cluster in the 1540s due to records of the export of wolfskins. The next cluster is in the 1650s and 1660s and this reflects the Cromwellian focus on wolves in Ireland. The

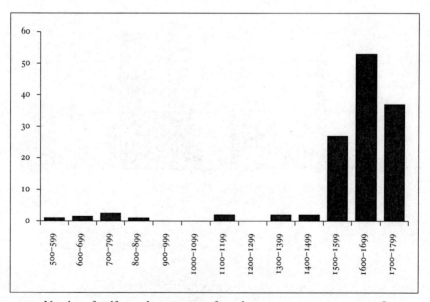

5.1 Number of wolf records per century from documentary sources, AD500–1800.

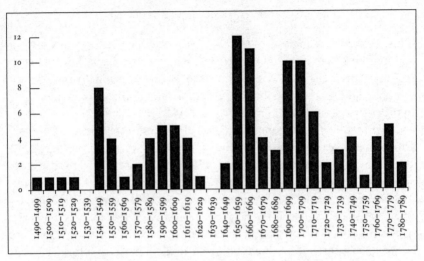

5.2 Number of wolf records per decade from documentary sources, AD1490–1790.

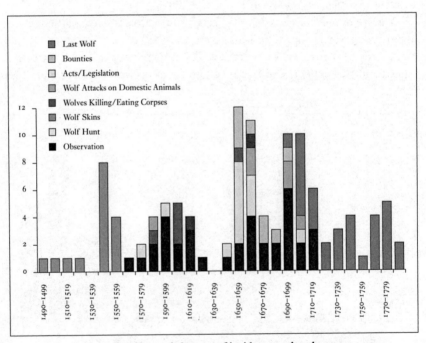

5.3 Breakdown of wolf records by type of incident per decade, AD1490–1790.

next peak occurs in the two decades of the 1700s and the 1710s and represents a cluster of notices of last wolves, some of them quite premature in claiming that they were the last wolves in Ireland. They probably believed their claims at the time but were proved wrong again and again as wolves were killed throughout most of the eighteenth century.

More insight into the nature of the documentary records can be achieved if the records are broken down by type (fig. 5.3). An eight-fold classification system was devised and the categories are observation of wolves, hunting of wolves, wolfskins, wolves killing humans and/or eating or disinterring corpses, wolf attacks on domestic animals, parliamentary acts and legislation dealing with wolves, notices of bounties paid and, finally, notices of last wolves at various scales. All of the records from 1490 up to 1559 relate to the export of wolfskins from Ireland to Bristol. Much work remains to be done on the Bristol custom books to extract all the wolfskin data, and what is presented here is a few records that have already been published and about which there is now some doubt.[73] This doubt is due to the recent publication of eleven of the port books from between 1503 and 1601, which identify far fewer wolfskins.[74]

From 1560 to 1699, most records of wolves are of the simple observation type, peaking with six in the 1690s. There are a few exceptions to this, however. In the decade of the 1600s, for example, there were three different records of wolves killing people, including injured soldiers after the Battle of Kinsale in 1601. In the 1650s, there were six records of wolf hunts being carried out and this is reflective of the Cromwellian obsession with exterminating wolves in Ireland. The decade of the 1660s has four observation records as well as three records of the hunting of wolves, two records of wolf attacks on humans and one record each of legislation and a bounty payment. From 1700 onwards, the remaining wolf records are dominated by records of last wolves, with the exception of the 1700s and 1710s, when a few observation records still occur. From 1720 onwards, only last wolf records occur and this shows that the wolf population was in severe decline. These records usually consist of the killing of the last wolf in a particular area, county or region, or Ireland as a whole.

The spatial distribution of the wolf records also shows some very interesting patterns (table 5.2). Firstly, the records essentially comprise two components, the first of which consists of very generalized locations – either Ireland as a whole or a province or a region consisting of multiple counties. The second component is made up of records where identification of the location is at the county level or a specific place. At the generalized level, the recorded location is Ireland forty-one times, Munster four times, Ulster three times, West Connacht twice, Connacht once and west and central Ireland once.

Table 5.2 Locations of documentary wolf records by frequency (see text for details).

Location	Up to 1786	After 1786	Location	Up to 1786	After 1786
Ireland	41		Co. Tyrone	3	1
Co. Cork	16		West Connacht	2	
Co. Waterford	11		Co. Clare	2	
Co. Antrim	7		Co. Offaly	2	
Co. Dublin	6		Connacht	1	
Co. Down	5		West and central Ireland	1	
Co. Wicklow	5		Co. Armagh	1	
Munster	4		Co. Carlow	1	
Co. Derry	4	1	Co. Galway	1	
Co. Kerry	4	3	Co. Kilkenny	1	
Co. Mayo	4		Co. Laois	1	
Co. Wexford	4		Co. Meath	1	
Ulster	3		Co. Monaghan	1	
Co. Kildare	3		Co. Sligo	1	
Co. Leitrim	3		Co. Tipperary	1	

At the county level (and this includes specific locations which have been aggregated up to county level), Co. Cork is most dominant with sixteen, mostly observational, records. This is followed by Co. Waterford with eleven records, almost all due to the export of wolfskins to Bristol from a number of ports in this county. These wolves were trapped in the great forests of Munster, which existed well into the seventeenth century. The next is Co. Antrim with seven records, followed by Dublin with six, and Down and Wicklow with five records each. Antrim features because of the similar survival of some of the great Ulster forests into the seventeenth century and the presence of mountains. The role of mountains and forest areas in Antrim, Dublin, Down and Wicklow was probably the critical factor in the number of records from these areas.

Remarkably, there are no records of wolves in eight Irish counties. Six of them occur in a block from Westmeath in the east to Donegal in the northwest, including Longford, Roscommon, Cavan and Fermanagh. One common feature that may go some way to explaining why there are no wolf records from these areas is the existence of extensive bog areas where there would have been few people and possibly little prey for the wolves. In addition, there are two outliers – Louth on the east coast and Limerick in the mid-west. It must be noted, however, that just because no records of wolves have been found for these counties, it does not mean that wolves were not present there. This is a fundamental problem when building a dataset from a vast variety of historical sources covering different locations and time periods. It is impossible to know what is missing and the discovery of one historical document with wolf references could alter this pattern considerably. The most surprising of the eight counties without wolf records is Donegal, given its diverse and mountainous landscape and even today its wilderness areas like at Glenveagh National Park and the fact that it has at least five place-names (esp. Breagh) related to wolves.

WOLF INCIDENTS POSSIBLY LATER THAN 1786

While most sources agree that there were no wolves in Ireland after 1786 at the latest, there is some evidence to suggest that a wolf was killed in Co. Kerry in 1790 and another in the Sperrin Mountains, Co. Tyrone, in 1810.[75] The Sperrins in particular had many traditions of wolves.[76] Of the 1810 claim, Fairley stated that when he contacted the source, he was unable to verify the information.[77] Local tradition recalls that the last wolf was killed in the 1800s in the mountains near Annascaul Lake in Co. Kerry.[78] A farmer claimed that the last wolf in the Dingle Peninsula was killed *c.*1829, but could offer no proof of this.[79]

Even as late as 1899 in an article in the *Spectator* entitled 'The British wolf', it is stated that

> It is just barely possible indeed that an isolated specimen or two of the breed may yet exist among the pathless wilds of Connemara, or some equally savage district – a report of the kind was current about two years ago – and may one day astonish us with an authentic discovery.[80]

This seems extremely unlikely, and the report of a couple of years previously most likely refers to domestic dogs that had gone feral. This might also explain some or all of the later sightings. One could speculate that if wolves had survived down to the Great Famine of the 1840s, they could still be with us today due to the massive and tragic population decline and abandonment of many upland and marginal areas, which would have allowed room for wolf expansion once again.

WOLF-DOGS IN IRELAND

According to James Ware, 'in Ireland, there are hounds which from their hunting of wolves are called wolf-dogs, being creatures of great strength and size and a fine shape'.[81] The Irish wolf-dog was a distinct race from the Scotch Hound or wolf-dog, which resembled the Irish breed in size and courage, but differed from it having a sharper muzzle and pendent ears.[82] Considerable research has been carried out on the Irish wolf-dog and the Irish wolfhound. Tradition relates that the boat which bore St Patrick away from his slavery on Mt Slemish carried a consignment of wolf hounds for sale in France.[83] Perhaps the Irish wolf-dog is what is alluded to by Quintus Aurelius Symmachus in AD393, when he states that seven dogs of great size were sent in iron cages from Ireland to Rome for his son's games and were exhibited in the circus, where they excited admiration on account of their strength and fierceness:[84]

> In order to win favour of the Roman people for our questor, you have been a generous and diligent provider of novel contributions to our shows, as is proved by your gift of seven Irish dogs. All Rome viewed with wonder, and fancy they must have been brought hither in iron cages.[85]

The Irish wolf-dogs made special gifts for the likes of the early Romans and the Great Mogul and were among the cargo of the boat that took St Columba from Ireland to France.[86] Indeed, St Columba is sometimes depicted with a wolfhound watching over a flock a sheep. Fergus Kelly notes that the earliest references to the massive Irish wolfhound are from the sixteenth century and that the archaeological evidence of the Early Christian period shows no dog bones larger than those of a modern Alsatian.[87]

Based mainly on their reputation, there was still a demand for wolves during the Tudor period, and this ultimately led to their destruction.[88] The dogs were normally exported in pairs for breeding purposes. Other dogs that are still in existence and which were formerly used to hunt wolves (and were specifically bred for that purpose) include the Borzoi, which is considered the Russian wolf-dog. These were usually set in twos or threes to course individual wolves.

No absolutely reliable distinction between the skeletal remains of the wolf and the large Irish wolfhound has yet been identified, but the angles of the eye-sockets differ slightly and could give a basis for differentiation, as could the dimensions of molar teeth.[89] Modern DNA analysis could probably resolve this problem. In a letter from Henry VIII to the lord deputy and council of Ireland, his majesty takes notice of the suit of the duke of Albuquerque, of Spain (of the privy council to Henry VIII) on behalf of the Marquis Desarrya and his sons that it might please his majesty to grant to the said marquis and his son, and the longer liver of the them, yearly, out of Ireland, two goshawks, and four wolf-hounds and commands the deputy for the time being to order the delivery of the hawks and hounds, and to charge the cost to the treasury.[90]

This represents a very significant commitment in terms of the export of four Irish wolfhounds a year. In the state papers for Ireland for November 1562, the Irish chieftain Shane O'Neill is recorded as sending to Queen Elizabeth through Robert Dudley, earl of Leicester, a present of two horses, two hawks and two Irish wolf-dogs.[91] Campion, writing in 1570, states that the Irish 'are not without wolves or greyhounds to hunt them; bigger of bone and limme than a colt'.[92] Sir John Perrott, who was lord deputy of Ireland from January 1584 to July 1588, sent to Sir Francis Walsingham, then secretary of state in London, a brace of good wolf-dogs, one black and one white. In 1596, an adventurous soldier named Gervaise Markham wrote that 'the long shaggy-haired, great-boned greyhounds are held most proper for vermin or wild beasts' – including the wolf and the fox.[93] Clearly the greyhound he is referring to is an Irish wolf-dog. In 1608, Irish wolfhounds were sent from Ireland by Captain Esmond of Duncannon to Gilbert, seventh earl of Shrewsbury.[94] There were hounds in Ireland which, due to their like of hunting wolves, were called wolf-dogs and were described as being creatures of great strength and size and a fine shape.[95] Due to over-export, they were becoming scarce even by the end of the sixteenth century, despite the large wolf population. They were also used for deer hunting and for guard duties against wolves. Abroad, they were thought fair and fierce and were also used for hunting wild boar, a very dangerous quarry.

In his history of the Irish wolf-dog, Hogan states that by the end of the seventeenth century the original type was almost extinct.[96] He goes on to describe them as fair, sleek hounds that were often pure white and bigger of bone and limb than a colt. The modern breed is the tallest dog in existence, although dogs from other breeds may hold the individual record. There is a record of a request by Guiciardini to the earl of Essex, who was looking for some Irish wolf-dogs for the purpose of wild boar hunting in 1596. Essex's role as a point of contact for sourcing dogs is underlined by a letter to him from Henry IV of France wanting the same.[97]

Irish wolfhounds were probably tall, rough greyhounds of extraordinary size and power, but Allen notes that the types used in ancient times differed considerably; some were more like mastiffs and some more like greyhounds.[98] This may indicate that there was no definitive Irish wolfhound breed and that the modern Irish wolfhound may not be truly representative of what went before it.

The importation of Irish wolf-dogs into Spain occurred in the seventeenth and eighteenth centuries, where they were employed in keeping wolves in check.[99]

> The common wolf is rare because few sheep are kept or because the country being overspread with farmsteads the animals are chased and killed as soon as they are sighted, and for this work the hounds brought into this country from Ireland are excellent.[1]

Although this reference does not specifically refer to wolfhounds, it seems most likely that this is what they were referring to. Irish wolf-dogs were also exported to the Far East, where they were regarded in high esteem. In 1617, during an interview between the emperor Jahangir and Sir Thomas Roe, Jahangir requested two tall Irish greyhounds (that is, wolf-dogs). Apparently, one of the Irish greyhounds had his head shot off.[2]

Many Irish wolf-dogs were exported to England in the sixteenth, seventeenth and eighteenth centuries.[3] Exportation appears to have progressed too fast, however, threatening the breed with extermination.[4] In 1652, a council order of Cromwell's government prohibited the export of wolf-dogs.[5] In November 1667, George Rawdon wrote to Viscount Conway explaining that he was on the lookout for a good Irish wolf-dog.[6] Another letter, by the secretary of the first duke of Ormond, lord lieutenant of Ireland, written on 11 March 1678 explains that

> I lately received commands from the earle of Ossory to putt you in mind of two wolf-dogs and a bitch wch his Lop. wrote to you about the king of Spayne, he desires they may be provided and sent wth all convenient speed, and that two dogs and a bitch be also gotten for the king of Sweeden.[7]

Revd J. Ovington, who made a voyage to Surat in the year 1689, relates that a couple of Irish wolf-dogs were so prized in Persia, that they were taken as a welcome and admired present by the emperor (Shah) himself. 'Two more of which (which were given to me by the earl of Inchequin when we put into Kingsale after the voyage) I disposed of to the East India Company, who dispatched them in their ships immediately to the Indies, to be there bestowed on some of the Eastern Courts'.[8]

Irish wolf-dogs were much valued and were often mentioned in contemporary correspondence as forming most acceptable gifts, and some of the people mentioned as receiving them include Cardinal Richelieu, the Shah of Persia and the Great Mogul, prior to the 1652 order banning their export.[9] The wolf-dog declined with the extermination of its natural quarry but retained its fierceness long after it was required for hunting wolves. There is a brief description of an Irish wolf-dog as recorded in the *London Gazette* of 27 March 1684, in which Gabriel Beranger describes them as seen in Connaught. He notes that they were amazingly large, white with black spots, but of the make and shape of the greyhound, only the head and neck were somewhat large in proportion.[10]

The long grey hounds that John Dunton saw bring deer to bay in Co. Galway in the 1690s seemed to him to be wolf-dogs that were very large and very fast and hunted by sight, which was a unique attribute. Dunton was astonished on entering a house to find 'nine-brace of wolfe doggs or the long Irish greyhound which were subsequently used for stag hunting'.[11]

Cox, writing in 1721, notes that 'some dogs are very great, as the wolf-dog, which is shaped like a greyhound, but is much taller, longer and thicker ... which are strong, fleet and bear a natural enmity to the wolf ... great fierceness'.[12]

It is difficult to know when the Irish wolf-dog died out. Various suggestions have been made, but nothing is certain.[13] The present day Irish wolfhound was created during the nineteenth century from crossings between Scottish Deerhounds, Great Danes, Mastiffs and Borzois, also known as the Russian wolfhound.[14] So, out of all this, it is possible that there were three different dogs in Ireland noted for their stature and wolf hunting abilities and which were extremely valuable and desirable. The first wolf-dog was exported to Rome and elsewhere around the first millennium BC and AD, the second wolf-dog seems to be a replacement of this earlier one from medieval times, and the current Irish wolfhound is most likely a Victorian recreation of the medieval wolf-dog, but it is very hard to be definitive given the nature of the scattered historical references.

CHAPTER 6

Population estimates and wolf zoology from the historic data

INTRODUCTION

At the end of the last Ice Age, both man and wolf would have been in competition for the same types of prey. Gradually, associations built up between the two species. This might have occurred when wolf cubs were caught by hunters or from scavenging around human settlements. Wolves would have fitted in fairly easily into human society as groups of humans and wolf packs have similar social structures and behaviour patterns in some respects. Over time, a wide variety of types of dogs have been bred from this one wolf ancestor to produce the vast array of dog breeds that can be found today.[1]

POPULATION ESTIMATES FOR IRELAND

Clearly, one of the big issues that needs to be addressed is how many wolves were in Ireland at any particular time. As has already been shown, there were numerous sightings of wolves throughout Ireland, indicating that wolves were not very rare or confined to a small number of locations. There is abundant evidence that wolves formerly existed in great numbers in Ireland.[2] However, this haphazard data only gives a vague impression of wolf numbers, with barely one record every three or four years over the period 1400 to 1786.

As the population and the extent of open cultivated land increased, wolves became less numerous and were held in check; but during the wars of the reign of Elizabeth, when the country was almost depopulated, they increased enormously and became bolder and fiercer, so that we often find notices of their ravages in the literature of those times.[3]

Fortunately, a number of approaches are possible to try and derive more concrete wolf numbers in Ireland from 1492 onwards. The three approaches used are an examination of the export of wolfskins from Ireland to Britain and in particular the Bristol port-books starting in 1492, an assessment based on habitat availability in 1600 and, finally, an analysis of two bounty payments made for wolf kills in Ireland in 1655 or 1665 (the date depends on the interpretation of an almost illegible number) and from July 1649 to November 1656. All the estimates are calculated as conservatively as possible in order not to overstate the likely number of wolves in Ireland at various time periods.

The information for the first estimate comes from the port and custom books from Bristol and other key British trading ports with Ireland including Bridgewater, Liverpool and others.[4] These books contain detailed manifests of the goods of all the ships that docked in these ports. This was necessary as different products had different levels of tax associated with them. Wolfskins were recorded as a separate category, as were other animal pelts.

In summary, the Bristol accounts alone show an average of between 100 and 300 wolfskins exported from Ireland each year throughout the 1500s and in the centuries before this. However, in the tax year 1504–5 (April to March), a total of 398 wolfskins were exported to Bristol, of which 103 arrived on English vessels and 295 on Irish vessels. Of the latter, a boat called the *Magdalen* of Waterford docked on 25 June. The list of its cargo includes 35 wolfskins valued at 4*s*. 4*d*., with a subsidy of 2½*d*. The value of the wolfskins was given as 1½*d*. each. By 1553, the value of each wolfskin had risen substantially to 8*d*., along with otter and pine marten skins, which were also highly prized.[5]

Most astonishingly, in the tax year 1558–9 (April to March), a total of 961 wolfskins were imported from Ireland into the port of Bristol alone at a total value of £32 1*s*. 4*d*. For 1558, 731 wolfskins were exported through four ports in Ireland: Cork with 321 wolfskins; Youghal with 160; Waterford with 149; and Ross with 101.[6] As discussed above, however, some doubt has recently been raised in relation to these figures: it is possible that they refer to fox skins rather than wolfskins.[7] The customs books indicate that the annual number of wolfskins ranged between two and eighteen, far below the numbers outlined above.[8] Unfortunately, none of the eleven customs books overlap with the earlier work, so until a recheck of these volumes is carried out, it is unclear what the true numbers of wolfskin exports were.[9] In addition, the last four customs books for the tax years 1563–4, 1575–6, 1594–5 and 1600–1 show not one wolfskin imported into Bristol from Ireland. This is in stark contrast to the earlier work.[10]

The numbers for exports fall off at the close of the sixteenth century due to two factors. The first is the destruction of large areas of the

Munster woods, where they were mainly caught, and the second is the general trade depression towards the end of the Tudor period. This depression mostly affected the population and trade of the areas around Munster towns such as Cork, Youghal, Waterford and Ross, which were identified as the most important centres for the distribution of wild animal skins, including wolfskins.[11]

Some simple assumptions need to be made in order to convert these figures into a population estimate.[12] Firstly, after 1600 there is still a considerable wolf population in Ireland, as evidenced by the documentary records of wolf sightings and by the substantial Cromwellian bounties offered for wolf kills in the mid-1600s. Secondly, in order to sustain that level of wolfskin export without a population collapse, as happens towards the end of the 1600s and into the 1700s, there must have been a sustainable breeding population unaffected by the hunting of wolves. Given the average yearly exports of between 100 and 300 wolfskins and the occasional figure outside this range, it is safe to assume a population at least double the higher average figure of 300, to give a minimum population of 600 wolves. Allowing for the occasional higher figure recorded and the exceptional year of 1588–9 when 961 wolfskins were exported, it is safe to push this minimum figure up to around 750 wolves and possibly as high as 1,000. Based on the more recent work, however, exported wolfskins seem to have been rarer and relatively expensive and the numbers would only justify a wolf population in Ireland of at most several hundred.[13]

A number of additional factors add to the validity of the higher estimates.[14] The first is the likelihood that not all wolfskins were exported, and that some were retained for domestic use (clothing and medicinal purposes) or were not in a fit state to be used at all. The second factor is that it is not clear whether the wolfskins exported were all adults or included juveniles and cubs. Certainly, if they were all adult wolves this would suggest a higher population figure as it takes wolves two years to reach maturity. Thirdly, only records from Bristol and a small number of other key trading ports were examined, whereas it is likely that some wolf-skins were sent to other British ports and possibly even European ports.

The fur of the wolf was formerly used for trimming robes, and was employed for this purpose at least as late as the Elizabethan period (1558–1603).[15] Wolfskins were mentioned in 1661 in a customs roll of Charles II, when two ounces of silver were paid for twenty of them. The value of a wolfskin in Wales, as fixed by the code of laws made by Howel Dha in the ninth century, was 8*d*. In 1868, the State of Minnesota paid $11,300 for wolf scalps at the rate of $10 each.[16] The trade in wolf fur continues to

6.1 Map of forest cover in Ireland, *c.*1600
(after McCracken, 1971).

some extent in Canada, Alaska, China
and Russia, but wolf fur never became
popular across Europe.[17]

The second assessment is based
on the state of the Irish landscape
around 1600 and human population
levels. This combination will roughly
indicate the extent of habitat available for wolves to occupy and, coupled
with information on the ecological
requirements of wolf packs, particularly from the USA, will indicate a
range of wolf numbers that could be
supported.

A detailed assessment of woodland in Ireland around 1600 from the
documentary records estimated that the total cover was around 12.5 per
cent (fig. 6.1). These woodlands occurred primarily in river valleys due to
the heavy nature of the soil and the resulting difficulties in cultivation
using the technology of the time. Tracts of woodland also occurred in the
more isolated regions of the north-west, west and south-west and in parts
of the north-east and south-east. Woodland was relatively scarce immediately around Dublin, with the exception of parts of the Wicklow
Mountains.[18] They were also scarce in the north central part of Ireland, as
far west as Galway city and Killala. There were no vast areas of untouched
woodland, but such as existed were of considerable size. This area by no
means represents the total area available for wolves, as at least a further 20
per cent of the country remained uncultivated, including mountains, bogs
and exposed limestone areas.

It must also be noted that just like modern urban foxes, wolves were
seen near and in some cases in cities at this time. In 1652, measures were
taken for the destruction of wolves in the barony of Castleknock,
Co. Dublin.[19] The documentary evidence also shows that wolves were
regularly found in cultivated areas. This indicates that wolves were also
surviving in areas with human populations and to that, to some extent,
they showed a lack of fear of humans.

The human population of Ireland at this time is estimated to be of the
order of 1 to 1.5 million.[20] Given the total land area of the island is

84,440km², this gives a maximum population density of 17 per km², which is very low. The 2002 population density was 46 per km². In addition, the population was by no means evenly distributed.²¹ This suggests that large tracts of Ireland were still in an uncultivated or relatively natural state, with low human populations. Coupled with the adaptability of wolves, this generates an estimate of the minimum available habitat of roughly a third of the land area of Ireland or around 27,500km². To convert this crude estimate into a possible wolf population level, some further calculations have to be made. Based on US data, pack sizes normally average between 5 and 10 individuals, although larger packs have been identified.²² In addition, wolf packs in the US have an average range of 350km² and a maximum range of 560km².

Firstly, a conservative figure is calculated based on the maximum range of a wolf pack. This was obtained by dividing this figure (the maximum range) into the estimated available Irish habitat. This calculation indicates a population of fifty packs of between five and ten individuals or an overall population of between 250 and 500 wolves. Even taking the lower figure of 250, this is easily a viable breeding population. Secondly, a less conservative estimate was calculated based on average range size. This resulted in a population estimate of seventy-eight packs of between five and ten individuals, or a total population of between 390 and 780 wolves, again well over the threshold for a sustainable viable breeding population.²³

The third wolf population estimate is based on a summary bounty payment from 1655 or 1665. In 1652, the commissioners of the revenue of the Cromwellian government in Ireland set enormous bounties on wolves. These were £6 for a female, £5 for a male, £2 for a hunting juvenile and 10s. for a cub.²⁴ It had long been a custom in England and Scotland to pay bounties on wolf kills. As early as 1167, the bishopric of Hereford, which at that time was vested in the king, paid out 10s. for three wolves captured in that year. In 1621, the price paid in Sutherlandshire in Scotland for the killing of one wolf was £6 13s. and 4d.²⁵

In 1655 or 1665, a total of £243 5s. 4d. was paid out by the revenue commissioners for wolf kills in Galway, Mayo, Sligo and part of Leitrim that was formerly within the precinct of Galway.²⁶ Unfortunately, no further breakdown of this figure is given. It must also be noted that this payment may have included some costs associated with hunting wolves, although there is no clear evidence to indicate the extent of this.

So, taking this figure and breaking it down, if all the wolf kills were female this would indicate a total of forty; if all male, this would indicate a total of forty-nine; if all were hunting juveniles, then this figure would represent 124 wolves; and if all were cubs, then this figure would represent 681 wolves. Obviously, the wolf kills would consist of a mixture of all four types, particularly as it is likely that individual packs would be targeted for extermination en masse. It is therefore conservatively suggested that this bounty represents a figure of between seventy-five and 150 wolf kills in that year in that part of Ireland.

As this area covers just under 14,000km², estimating that 25 per cent of the land area of Leitrim is included, then it is possible to extrapolate for the country as a whole assuming similar levels of wolf kills per unit area. This yields a possible total of between 460 and 920 wolf kills in that year. These estimates clearly indicate a sustainable and viable breeding population of wolves, as to sustain these losses the number of wolves must be well in excess of these figures (the more conservative one of 460 or the higher one of 920). Using Polish figures for a similar calculation for the UK, it is estimated that the wolf population in Britain (England, Scotland and Wales) was probably as high as 6,600 during the Mesolithic period.[27] Applying this approach to Ireland would yield a figure of 2,400, given the relative size of Ireland. However, on consideration of the lack of large prey species in Ireland (except wild boar), a figure of one thousand or fewer would be far more realistic.

The fourth estimate is based on a summary bounty total paid out from July 1649 to November 1656. For this period of seven and a half years, the total amount paid over for wolf kills in Ireland was £3,847 5s., an enormous amount of money by the standards of the time.[28] Again, some caution must be exercised with this figure, as some of this money may have been used to purchase wolf hunting and trapping equipment, although there is no clear evidence of this.

To use this figure to derive annual wolf kills and ultimately estimates of annual wolf populations, it was assumed that the same amount of bounty was paid out each year over the seven and a half years. This gives an annual bounty of £513. If all the wolf kills were female, then this figure would reflect eighty-five wolves; if all were male then this would rise to 103; if all were hunting juveniles this would represent 256 wolves; and if all were cubs this would rise to 1,436. Again, the total bounty each year would be for a mixture of all four as it is likely that most kills would be associated with the targeting and extermination of individual packs. It is suggested that this bounty would conservatively represent an annual wolf kill of between 225 and 400 individuals. This would indicate that for the population of wolves to be sustained over this period, the overall wolf population was higher by some margin. This would be despite the likelihood that higher numbers of wolf kills would have occurred at the start of the period, declining towards the end as the effects of hunting started to make wolves scarcer. It is conservatively suggested that a factor of two might be applied to the number of wolf kills to give some estimate of the overall population. This allows for the fact that this phase of wolf extermination was not totally successful and there were residual wolf populations around the country. If this factor of two is used, then an estimate of the total wolf population for Ireland was between 450 and 800.

There is one small anomaly that must be noted with this bounty figure. This is that the earliest date known for the instigation of the Cromwellian bounties is 1652, yet the bounty figure above dates back to July 1649. There are two possible explanations: firstly, that the bounties were being paid in advance of the legislation; or, secondly, that bounties were paid retrospectively back to 1649 after the legislation was enacted.

Based on the four estimates outlined above – three from direct wolf data and one from a habitat assessment – it is safe to assume that throughout the 1500s and as late as the 1650s or 1660s, Ireland had a considerable wolf population capable of sustaining considerable annual losses. The evidence suggests a wolf population of somewhere between 500 and 1,000 throughout this period, the latter figure being more likely.

It is even suggested by some authors that as a result of the military campaigns in Ireland, particularly the Cromwellian Wars of 1641–52 and the associated devastation of much of the country and loss of population, wolf numbers were again on the increase.[29] Wolves were taking advantage of the desolation that was occurring to such an extent that they were becoming common even in the outskirts of Dublin, so much so that in December 1652 a wolf hunt was organized at Castleknock.[30] This shows the resilience of the wolf population and their ability to rapidly replace population losses.

From 1683 onwards, the rarity of wolves is mentioned more and more and it is clear that by this time the effect of the bounties and all the other changes that had occurred was impacting significantly on the wolf population in Ireland.[31] In the Barrett–Lennard Papers, there is reference to fourteen wolves inhabiting Slieve Beagh in north Monaghan as late as November 1696.[32] It is remarkable and confusing, considering the number of claims for last wolves in various counties between 1700 and 1712, indicating a period of significant fragmentation and decline of the Irish wolf population.

ASPECTS OF THE ZOOLOGY OF THE IRISH WOLF WITH
REFERENCE TO PREFERRED HABITATS AND BREEDING

Wolves prefer to have a variety of habitat types within their range. They need a supply of water and food and most importantly a secluded area for breeding purposes.[33] When fully grown, individual wolves can be up to 1.7m in length, of which 1–1.25m is the torso. Adult males can weigh up to 57kg; females a little smaller. On average, wolves live for ten years but can live up to sixteen.[34] One of the most important characteristics of these animals is that they operate in packs. Pack sizes vary depending upon a number of factors, the primary one being a regular food supply. Packs normally consist of between five and twenty individuals. In the Mercantour area of the French Alps, three packs of five, nine and thirteen wolves were identified in 1999.[35] In Alaska, packs in excess of thirty individuals occur, but packs in Europe are far smaller, and some wolves actually operate alone.[36]

The wolf pack is controlled by a dominant pair and only they are allowed to breed. This pair is known as the alpha male and alpha female. Wolves reach breeding age at three years, have a short gestation period of two months and usually produce between four and six cubs. They have excellent reproductive rates and can double their population annually, depending on the availability of suitable habitats and prey. The minimum sustainable breeding population is estimated at fifty individuals.[37]

A seventeenth-century description of wolves provides some interesting insights into their behaviour and methods of hunting them:

> There is no beast which runeth faster than the wolf, and holdeth wonderfully also. When he is hunted with hounds he flieth not far before them; and unless he be coursed with greyhounds or mastiffs he keepeth the covert like the bear and boar and especially the beaten ways within. Night is the usual time of his preying, though hunger will force him to prey by day. They are more subtle and crafty if more can be than the fox or any other beast. When they are hunted they will take all their advantages at other times they will run over hastily, but keep themselves in breath and force always.
>
> A wolf will stand up a whole day before a good kennel of hounds, unless that greyhounds or wolf-dogs course him. If he stands at bay, have a care of being bitten by him, for being then mad, the wound is desperate and hard to be cured. … and therefore all means should be used to destroy them, as by hunting at force, or with greyhounds or

mastiffs, or caught in gins and snares but they had need be strong. ...
When anyone would hunt the wolf, he must train him by these
means: first let him look out some fair place, a mile or more from the
great woods, where there is some close standing, to place a brace of
good greyhounds in, if need be the which should be closely
environed and some pond of water by it. There he must kill a horse,
that is worth little, and take the four legs thereof, and carry them into
the woods and forests adjoining, then let four men take a leg of the
beast and at his horse tail draw it along the paths and ways in the
woods, until they come back again to the place where the carcase of
the said beast lieth, there let them lay down their trains. Now when
the wolves go out in the night to prey, they will follow the scent of
the train till they come to the carcase where it lieth. Then let those
who love the sport, with their huntsmen come early and privately
near the place and if they are discernible as they are feeding, in the
first place let them consider which way will be the fairest course for
the greyhounds, and place them accordingly, and as near as they can
let them forestall with their greyhounds the same way that the wolves
did or are flying either then or the night before; but if the wolves be
in the coverts near the carrion that was laid for them to feed upon,
then let there be hewers set around the coverts to make a noise on
every side but only that where the greyhounds do stand, and let
them stand thick together, making what noise they can to force them
to the greyhounds. Then let the huntsman go with his lead hound
and draw from the carrion to the thickets side where the wolves have
gone in, and their the huntsman shall call off the third part of his
best hounds; for the wolf will sometimes hold a covert a long time
before he will come out.

The huntsman must hold near in to the hounds blowing hard and
encouraging them with their voice for many hounds will strain
courtesy at this chase, although they are strong and fit for all other
chases. When the wolf cometh to the greyhounds, they who hold
them will do well to suffer the wolf to pass the first rank until he
cometh further, and let the last rank let slip their greyhounds full in
the face of the wolf, and at the same instant let all other ranks let slip
also, so that the first rank staying him but ever so little, he may be
assaulted on all sides at once, and by that means they shall the more
easily take him.

It is best entering of hounds at young wolves, which are not yet
past half a year or a year old, for a hound will hunt such more willing

and with less fear than an old wolf, or you may take wolves alive in engines, and breaking their teeth, enter your hounds at them. ... The reward of the dogs is thus; when they have bit and shaked the dead wolf, let the huntsman then open his belly straight along, and taking out his bowels, let him throw in bread, cheese and other scraps and so let the dogs feed therein.[38]

Extensive woodland cover would have suited wolves and other native mammals.[39] Wolves do not have their litters deep underground like the fox. Foxes and wolves are natural enemies and it has been observed that a fox may lay a herb called a sea-onion at the mouth of its den, which acts as a wolf deterrent. Wolves so hate this herb that they are not to be found anywhere it grows and Cox goes on to provide a detailed account of the mating habits of the wolves and the rearing of pups or whelps as he calls them.

First as to their nature. They go a clicketting in February and continue in that manner ten or twelve days. Where many wolves are, many will follow one bitch as dogs will follow a bitch that is salt, but she will be only lined with one.

A notable story I have heard when I was in Ireland and attested for a truth by the inhabitants: that a bitch wolf will suffer a great many of the male to follow her, and will carry them after her sometimes eight or ten days without meat, drink or rest; and when they are tired that they cannot travel farther, she will first lie down, then will the rest follow her example: when she perceives that they are all asleep, and through weariness snore, then will she arise and awake that wolf which she observed to follow her most, and having so done entice him with her far from the rest, and suffer him to line her, thereafter awaking and finding how she hath cunningly deluded them, they all instantly on her companion who hath been beforehand with them, and revenge themselves on him by depriving him of his life; which verifies the proverb: never wolf yet saw his sire.

Their whelps are able to ingeader at twelve months end, at which age they part with their dam, that is when those teeth are grown which they cast the first half year, and being grown, they never shed them again: and here see their gratitude, though bloody creatures after they preyed for themselves if they chance to meet their dam or sire (for Turberville doth not believe the aforesaid story) they will fawn upon them and lick them, rejoicing at the sight of them.

The dog will never bring any of his prey to his whelps till he hath filled his own belly, whereas the bitch will not eat a bit till she hath served them first; they go none (that is, nine) weeks with whelp, and sometimes a little longer, and grow salt but once a year.[40]

ASPECTS OF THE ZOOLOGY OF THE IRISH WOLF WITH REFERENCE TO FOOD REQUIREMENTS

It is likely that wolves preyed on the giant deer (*Megaloceros giganteus*) as a major source of food, but it is probable that they picked off any old and ill animals that were unable to keep up with their herds. During the rutting season, the male deer's enormous antlers would have been a formidable weapon against a wolf attack.[41] Each year in Sweden, the population of approximately eighty wolves is responsible for the death of about a thousand moose, also known as elk (*Alces alces*), an animal similar in size to the giant deer.[42] They also target reindeer (*Rangifer tarandus*) as a significant food resource.[43] Wild boar would also have been available as a source of food in Ireland right up to the medieval period, unlike the two deer species.

In the initial post-glacial period, the countryside was teeming with prey suitable for wolves. Later, when humans brought cattle and sheep into the country, the wolves took these animals instead.[44] One important role that the wolf undertook was the control of the grazers, in particular deer and wild boar (*Sus scrofa*). If left unchecked, these grazers and others can do considerable damage to the forest by eating saplings and stripping bark from young trees, thus inhibiting forest regeneration.[45]

Wolves are considered opportunistic feeders, but will primarily concentrate on big game where possible. In Ireland, this would have been deer and wild boar, but wolves will eat almost anything, including rodents, birds, reptiles, fish, crabs and even insects, worms and berries (pl. 8). Domesticated animals such as sheep, cattle and even horses are relatively easy prey for a hungry wolf pack.[46] We are all aware of the damage that a pack of stray dogs can do to a flock of sheep; imagine what a wolf pack is capable of doing in similar circumstances.[47] Wolves are persistent hunters, can travel long distances effortlessly and eventually wear down their prey and then pick off the weakest individual, even if this takes several days.

There is some discussion about the lack of prey that would have been available for wolves and other predators in Ireland once the giant deer and reindeer were gone. It seems likely now that red deer (*Cervus elaphus*) were not present in the initial post-glacial period, nor perhaps throughout much of the rest of that period. It turns out that they may not even be native to Ireland but were an introduced species that arrived in the last three millennia. This creates a conundrum. There were many predators: wolves; brown bear (*Ursus arctos arctos*); and lynx (*Lynx lynx*), for instance, but almost no large wild prey, with the exception of the wild boar.

Wolves were a danger to all types of cattle and will feed on carrion and vermin along with sheep, goats and pigs. If they attack a flock of sheep they will sometimes kill as many of them as they can before starting to feed.[48] It is claimed that in the five years up to 1998, wolves had killed 2,978 sheep in the French Alps alone.[49] The hunting prowess of wolves can be further demonstrated by the fact that even in captivity in Dublin Zoo they kill and eat wild birds that come into their enclosure (pl. 8). Remarkably, in Ethiopia the Ethiopian wolf (*Canis simensis*) is tolerated by shepherds as the wolves kill large numbers of rodents.[50]

One old wives' myth that has been dispelled is that wolves howl on the hunt and at the kill. This is not the case. They generally only howl to find each other or to remind other packs not to invade their territory, or sometimes just for the joy of it (pls 3, 7).[51] There is a small number of records of wolves being eaten by humans, most recently when Israeli authorities were forced to order a three-year ban on hunting after Thai guest workers were blamed for eating everything from the wild including wolves.[52]

WOLF ATTACKS ON HUMANS

Although rare in the record and disputed to a certain extent by some researchers on wolves, with the exception of attacks by rabid animals, there is a history of wolf attacks on humans even up the present day, with children being particularly vulnerable. Two studies on European wolf attacks between 1815 and 1965 and on global wolf attacks between 1923 and 1936 both failed to find a verifiable attack on humans.[53] The issue of coyote-wolf hybrid attacks confuses the issue. This is epitomized by the case of a 19-year-old woman who was walking alone in the Cape Breton Highland National Park in Nova Scotia, Canada, in October 2009 when she was attacked and killed by two coyote-wolf hybrids. Wolf attacks on humans are rare and are often mistaken for attempts by the wolves to kill the horses on which the humans were riding.[54]

In March 1348, the town of Split in Croatia was suffering from the Black Death. Wolves came down from the mountains into the plague-stricken city and attacked the survivors. In November 1348, in Styria, Austria, wolves came down from the mountains but subsequently fled back into the wilderness as if they understood they too were vulnerable to the Black Death.[55] As we saw above, in seventeenth-century Ireland, wolves also took advantage of humans weakened by hunger and illness, attacking the war-weary and famine-afflicted.[56] The last wolf in Scotland was apparently exterminated as a result of killing two children in Morayshire in 1743,[57] but this would seem to be far too late for the last Scottish wolf.[58] About the same time, in 1745, a man was killed by a wolf in Co. Mayo.[59]

Parish records from Sweden in the first half of the nineteenth century record several cases of fatal attacks by wolves, although no firm details are given.[60] There is only one report of a wolf attack on a man in a scientific journal and this occurred in Canada in 1942 and the details suggest that the animal was rabid. To substantiate this view that wolves are not a threat to humans, Fairley highlights the fact that in the wilderness of Algonquin Park in Ontario in Canada, where there is a high wolf density, thousands of children are allowed to camp every year.[61] Nonetheless, there is clear evidence that wolves killed at least seven children and injured more than a dozen people in the state of Uttar Pradesh in northern India over a three-month period in 2003. The suggested explanation for the attacks was that with dwindling forest the wolves are being pushed closer to villages in search of prey. With no food around, they first attack small animals and then children.[62] This area is notorious for wolf attacks on humans, especially children.[63]

There were attacks by a pack of wolves on fourteen people in villages of the Zaporizha region of eastern Ukraine over a three-day period in January 2005. One of the wolves was killed by a car and was found to be rabid. This supports the idea that rabid wolves are more likely to attack humans.[64] On 15 February 2005, the exceptionally cold winter drove wolves to attack humans for food, resulting in four deaths and twenty-two other people being bitten in Paktia Province in Afghanistan, close to its border with Pakistan.[65]

So the evidence of wolf attacks on humans is mixed. They are relatively rare and many are associated with rabid individuals. There is no doubt that attacks on humans by non-rabid wolves do occur, however, with children being the most vulnerable.

CHAPTER 7

Causes of the decline and extermination of the wolf in Ireland

INTRODUCTION

The decline and extermination of wolves in Ireland was by no means straightforward and there were many factors that eventually led to their demise. Not unsurprisingly, there is no reference to wolves being eaten as food as, throughout Europe, canines were considered unsuitable for human consumption. During the siege of Paris in 1870, however, virtually the whole animal population of the zoo was eaten, including wolves served in venison sauce[1] – a rather ironic choice of accompaniment, given that wolves usually hunt deer.

LEGISLATION DEALING WITH THE WOLF PROBLEM IN IRELAND

Possibly as early as the seventh century there is evidence that wolf-hunting was considered a public duty, to the point where certain individuals were obliged to hunt wolves once per week.[2] Prior to English rule, it was a sport of Irish chieftains to hunt the wolf, but there is no evidence of any attempt to exterminate them. The chieftains used wolf-dogs or wolfhounds to assist them. The practice was to kill a horse and trail it through the woods, eventually depositing it in a clearing. The hunters and their dogs then laid in wait for the wolves to turn up, at which time they were quickly killed. The fact that they were prepared to kill a horse in order to trap wolves shows how much of a menace they were considered.

Around 1185, permission to hunt wolves in Ireland was given by the English crown. As farming developed and more of the country was put under pasture, an inevitable conflict with the wolf population started to develop and to become a serious issue. As a result, legislation began to be brought in to deal with the conflict.[3] Under instruction from the English authorities, who took the view that Ireland could not be considered civilized with wolves roaming around the countryside, organized hunting of wolves took place.[4] This is especially the case as wolves had long disappeared from England, Wales and Scotland.

In a book of information compiled by Robert Legge in January 1584 and delivered to Sir John Perrott, the lord deputy of Ireland, it was suggested that leases for tenants should include provision for the trapping and killing of what were described as 'ravening and devouring wolves', and this was to be done with traps, snares or other devices.[5] This scheme does not appear to have been put into effect until many years later.[6]

In November 1611, under James I, an act for killing wolves and other vermin was put together but never passed. The act was to specify the days of hunting, the people who were to attend, who was to be the director and an inhibition on the use of arms. In addition, the deputy or principal governor was to prohibit such hunting if it was suspected as being a cover for more political activities.[7] This latter clause was in response to concerns expressed at the time that the act might be used by the Irish as an excuse for groups of them to go around the countryside fully armed, which, unsurprisingly, was not considered desirable by the English authorities.[8] Nonetheless, this act was passed.[9]

On 27 April 1652, a council order of Cromwell's government was made to prevent the export of Irish wolf-dogs on account of the growing wolf problem.[10] In 1653, Cromwell brought out a bill spelling out the necessity to hunt and destroy wolves. This included the specification of days and times for wolves to be hunted and the paying of bounties for each wolf head produced, based upon whether the wolf was female, male or cub. This upped the rate of destruction of wolves very significantly.[11] This legislation can be considered as one of the two most important factors in the extermination of wolves in Ireland. An order dated to 1659 from the Commonwealth records notes that toils (traps), snares and nets for catching wolves were provided from public money.[12]

In 1662, a bill of parliament was brought in to encourage the killing of wolves and foxes in Ireland.[13] The issue of wolf numbers was being dealt with by similar legislation across Europe. In Sweden, the 1664 Game Act required peasants of both sexes to act as beaters for wolf hunts on a regular basis, the only exceptions being priests and elderly widows.[14]

BOUNTIES AND BOUNTY HUNTERS

Wolf bounties were not new in the seventeenth century. Around AD800, Charlemagne established a special wolf-hunting force called the Louveterie in what was to become France. It was still in existence until 1789, was reformed in 1814 and carried on until the last wolf was killed in France in 1927.[15] In AD985, the English king, Edgar, imposed an annual tax on Wales of 300 wolfskins. This quickly led to the demise of wolves in Wales.[16] The use of bounties from the nineteenth century onwards in the USA led to the almost complete eradication of wolves from the lower forty-eight states by 1945.[17]

In 1610, rewards (unspecified) were given for the destruction of wolves.[18] A grant was made to Henric Tuttesham of Newmarket in England in 1614 to go to Ireland to destroy wolves, as recorded in the patent rolls of James I:

> The king, being given to understand the great loss and hindrance which rose in Ireland by the multitude of wolves in all parts of the kingdom, did by letters from Newmarket 26th November 1614 direct a grant be made by patent to Henric Tuttesham, who by petition had made offer to repair to Ireland, and there use his best skill and endeavour to destroy the said wolves, providing at his own charge, men, dogs, traps and engines and requires no other allowance save four nobles [about £3], for the head of every wolf, young or old and of every county, and to authorised to keep four men and twelve couple of hounds in every county for the next seven years.[19]

This represents a very significant professional attempt to eliminate wolves. Unfortunately, no information on how he got on with this task has been found. In 1621, the price paid in Sutherlandshire in Scotland for the killing of one wolf was £6 13s. 4d.[20]

As a result of the events of 1641 and the arrival of Cromwell, wolves increased in number to such an extent, and their ravages became so great, as to require state interference, and wolf hunters were appointed in various parts of Ireland.[21] Although wolf hunters were employed, they had little impact on wolf numbers.[22] They were employed by the Cromwellian government because there was a great fear that with so many wolves in Ireland the country could not be governed properly as potential settlers were unlikely to take the risk of farming there.

Lands lying only nine miles from Dublin were leased by the state in 1653, on condition that a hunt be established with a pack of wolfhounds for killing wolves. Part of the rent was to be discounted in wolves' heads, at the rate of the declaration of 29 June 1653:

Under this lease, Captain Edward Piers was to have all the state lands in the barony of Dunboyne, in the county of Meath, valued at £543 8s. 8d. at a rent greater by £100 a year than they then yielded in rent and contribution, for five years from 1st May following, on terms of maintaining at Dublin and Dunboyne three wolf-dogs, two English mastiffs, a pack of hounds of sixteen couple (three whereof to hunt the wolf only), a knowing huntsman and two men, and one boy and an orderly hunt to take place thrice a month at least. Captain Piers was to bring to the commissioners of revenue at Dublin a stipulated number of wolves' heads in the first year, and a diminishing number every year, but for every wolf head whereby he fell short of the stipulated number, £5 was to be defalked from his salary.[23]

It is clear from this that in order to take on such a lease, Captain Piers must have been sure of reaching the required number of wolves, otherwise the financial penalty was very high. As security against the performance of his duties, Piers had to deposit £100 annually in addition to his rent and he was to destroy at least fourteen wolves and sixty foxes over five years.[24] The reward for fox kills was 5s., far less than that for adult wolves.

The extermination of the wolf in Ireland along with other creatures considered dangerous to humans and their activities was primarily as a result of hunting and not landscape change.[25] To some extent, this would have been in keeping with the views of the time and a less developed understanding of the role of the landscape in maintaining species diversity. Wolf hunting with hounds required high levels of skill and endurance as hunts of three days were not unusual.[26]

DEFORESTATION AND HABITAT CHANGE

As woodland and scrub disappeared after AD1600, wolves were pushed to the brink of extinction, whereas previously they thrived as a result of lack of habitat pressure and small human population.[27] There is considerable debate as to the amount of woodland in Ireland in the seventeenth century.[28] Using a variety of historical and cartographic sources, a figure of less than 12.5 per cent forestry cover has been suggested.[29] Using similar figures from the Civil Survey of 1654–6, Oliver Rackham arrived at a figure of just 3 per cent.[30] This would have consisted of a combination of underwood and timber wood. A detailed analysis of the civil parishes in west Cork, based on the Civil Survey, suggests that the average woodland cover was around 6 per cent, which would have been enough for a self-sufficient community.[31]

Commercial exploitation of Irish woodland by English settlers was carried out during the seventeenth and eighteenth centuries, but a steady reduction in the area and density had been ongoing over the previous centuries. The woods had been depleted by a virtually self-sufficient rural society.[32] The demise of most of the remaining woodlands between 1600 and 1750 was the result of a number of factors, one of which was the removal of wolves, of which the new regime in Ireland was utterly intolerant.[33] During this period, the woodland would have been one of the last refuges of a wolf population that was declining and under pressure. The substantially forested Ireland in 1600 had by 1711 become a treeless wilderness and a net importer of timber. Deforestation was a major factor in the demise of not just the wolf but also different species of eagles and other birds, the Irish wild cat and other creatures.[34]

To the Elizabethans and the Jacobeans, the density of the forests in Ireland was to be deplored, on the one hand, because of their harbouring of wolves and woodkerne (Irish rebels) and later Tories. On the other hand, the forests were viewed positively because they could be very profitably cut down for timber during a time when it was in short supply in England and Wales.[35] Some of the destruction of woods was politically and militarily motivated and involved the burning of areas of impenetrable forest to get at Irish rebels. This also had a significant impact on wildlife, including wolves.[36]

The destruction of the remaining woods of Ireland in the sixteenth and seventeenth centuries deprived the wolf of its natural habitat, and the last wolves were killed in the early eighteenth century.[37] By the end of the seventeenth century, the old forests were no more, but the wolves were not yet extinct and war conditions had been favourable to their continued existence.[38] Although much reduced by the deforestation, wolves were still numerous even up to the outskirts of Dublin.

As the woods dwindled throughout the eighteenth century, the available habitat declined to a few isolated pockets insufficient to sustain wolf populations.[39] One by one, these populations died out as deforestation and hunting continued. They probably also felt the effects of inbreeding, which would have been a significant factor once wolf numbers had declined to a certain level. The relatively late extinction of the wolf in Ireland can be attributed to the longevity of the dense woodland cover and sparse human settlement in sizeable areas.[40]

Associated with deforestation was the creation of extensive tracts of farmland that we recognize today in a process known as enclosure and shiring.[41] The scale of transformation planned can be understood from an observation regarding the Maguire territory in Co. Fermanagh prior to shiring:

> The county of Fermanagh, sometimes Maguire's country, rejoice. Many undertakers, all incorporated in mind as one, they with their followers, seek and are desirous to settle themselves. Woe to the wolf and wood kerne! The island of Lough Erne shall have habitations, a fortified corporation, market towns and many new erected manors shall now so beautify her desolation that her inaccessible woods, with spaces made tractable, shall no longer nourish devourers, but by the sweet society of a loving neighbourhood, shall entertain humanity even in the best society.

It is possible that the destruction of the wildwood and not the bounties and hunting of the wolf was what finally drove them into their last mountain retreats.

HUMAN POPULATION CHANGE

Around 1600 the population of Ireland was estimated at not more than 1 million to 1.5 million and, with the exception of period of the Cromwellian Wars in the mid-1600s, the population carried on rising up to the Great Famine of the 1840s, when the population was at least 8 million and possibly much greater.[42] This low human population around 1600 would not have been much of a nuisance to the wolves.[43] The wolf population multiplied in the great tracts of land lying waste and deserted in all parts of Ireland in the seventeenth century; they increased until they became so serious a public nuisance, destroying sheep and cattle, that various measures had to be taken against them.

ATTITUDES

Wolves were plentiful throughout the medieval period and, although hunted on occasion, they were generally tolerated until about 1600, after which time they were systematically persecuted. This represented a significant change in attitudes, as space was no longer shared with wolves.[44]

There appears to have been a significant difference in the way wolves were viewed by the native Irish on the one hand, and by the new settlers on the other. The native Irish saw them as part of the natural landscape of the country, to be hunted on occasion (hence the existence of the Irish wolf-dog). Some native lords even kept them as pets, along with foxes, deer, badgers, hawks, crows and herons.[45] There was no determination to exterminate them from the landscape and the Brehon Laws acknowledged their existence and occasional predation on domesticated livestock.

The new settlers had a very different attitude and most were horrified to discover large numbers of wolves still roaming the countryside when they arrived in Ireland. They saw them as a threat to the kind of landscape they wished to create and set about eliminating them as quickly as possible. There were no thoughts of accommodating them.

This attitude persists down to the present day, when wolves are seen as a significant threat in many countries, including parts of the USA where they are increasing in numbers and range and the old animosities are rapidly re-emerging.[46]

CHAPTER 8

Final comments

INTRODUCTION

The wolf seems to have occupied a unique position within the natural and cultural history of Ireland, being seen as part of the ordinary wildlife of the country. It was looked to for strength and protection but at the same time was feared as an agent of evil. The wolf was seen as an intermediary between the physical and spiritual worlds in Pagan times – a tradition that survived in many places long into the Christian era. Although long gone physically, the wolf still permeates many aspects of Ireland's cultural history, albeit hidden from us and filtered through language and cultural change.

THE LOSS OF ONE OF OUR FOREMOST PREDATORS

Wolves were far more common than is generally realized and they almost survived right down to the present day. It is possible that wolves would still be around in Ireland if a viable population had survived down to the Great Famine, as the subsequent depopulation and abandonment of upland areas would have provided enough space for a small population of wolves to survive.

There were probably no more than a thousand wolves in Ireland from 1600 onwards. They were quite dispersed and people were used to having them around, even if not everyone was comfortable with this. The most likely date for the death of the last wolf in Ireland is 1786, when the sole survivor was killed on Mount Leinster on the Wexford/Carlow border. There is a surprising lack of drawings, paintings, detailed written descriptions and stuffed specimens; not even a head has survived. It is possible that one may yet turn up, most likely in a large house or hunting lodge in some attic or basement.

THE POSSIBILITY OF THE IRISH WOLF AS A UNIQUE SUB-SPECIES

As a result of being isolated for so long – maybe 10,000 years or more – it is possible that wolves in Ireland developed particular characteristics, becoming a distinctive sub-species, similar to the Irish stoat (*Mustela erminea hibernica*) and the Irish hare (*Lepus timidus hibernicus*). It is likely that the Irish hare may even be declared a species in its own right in the not too distant future, based on recent DNA analysis showing its uniqueness.[1] Many isolated wolf populations have become distinct sub-species. This process is helped by their high breeding capacity, the rapid turnover in generations and their response to local conditions.[2] It is unlikely that there would have been enough time for them to become a distinctive species, however.

The best way to test for any differences would be through a DNA examination of recent (medieval) wolf remains from Ireland, comparing them with existing European populations. Remarkably, no recent wolf bones, skulls or specimens have survived from which the necessary tests could be carried out. If the wolf had survived in Ireland to the Victorian period, there is no doubt that there would be some remains now, given their predilection for collecting all sorts of natural history specimens from fossils and rocks through to stuffed animals and birds and other natural specimens.

THE POSSIBILITY OF REINTRODUCTION

Reintroducing wolves in any area is a very emotive issue and one which few people do not have an opinion on. A lot of factors have to be considered and it is not just a case of turning up with a few packs of wolves and letting them loose in the landscape. The considerations include legal protection and ongoing monitoring, costs including a compensation scheme for farm animal losses, a suitable landscape including breeding areas, an adequate food supply and public attitudes.

Wolves are making a comeback where they are protected, including the lower forty-eight states of the USA and many European countries where they had been exterminated, including Germany and Sweden. They thrive, even in some areas with high human population numbers. As their numbers rise, they are coming back into conflict with farmers and other rural dwellers.[3]

There are a number of reasons why I would consider the reintroduction of wolves into Ireland as being extremely unlikely, currently and well into the future. Firstly, the landscape is radically different from the time when wolves were last around. Very little deciduous forest exists – extensive farming, vast networks of roads and other human structures now dominate our landscape. Almost no parts of the country remain untouched by humans and there is consequently a lack of a suitably large wilderness area. Even our biggest national park in Glenveagh is not sufficiently big or wild enough to sustain one wolf pack, not to mention the forty to fifty from different existing stocks that would be necessary to prevent in-breeding and maintain a viable population.

Over 20,000km² (over 7,800 square miles) would be needed to maintain a viable population of fifty individuals in a US context.[4] This area is more than half the size of Ireland, although it must be noted that in an Irish context the land requirements would be considerably less. Wolves are capable of doubling their population annually, given protected conditions; but this would mean that the new packs that would form would be forced to move out of the preserved area in search of their own territory. Currently, to sustain the existing wolf populations in Europe there is a need to preserve wild regional corridors of forest and mountain to help the migration of these wide-ranging mammals.[5]

Public attitudes would have to change enormously in order for a successful reintroduction to take place, particularly among rural dwellers, farmers and forestry workers, who would most likely come into contact with wolves. The difficulties with this aspect of the reintroduction into Ireland of the Golden Eagle (*Aquila chrysaetos*) and the White-Tailed Eagle (*Haliaeetus albicilla*) give an insight into this and should not be under-estimated.[6] In Scotland in 2004, a millionaire businessman, Paul Lister, who purchased a 23,000-acre estate, announced his intention of setting up an enclosed game reserve and restoring the native vegetation of Scotland and to populate this reserve with (up to twenty) wolves, bears, beaver and lynx. This plan was met with huge public opposition. Once operational, the game reserve would be used as a tourist venue similar to those in Africa.[7] In the main Spanish population of wolves in Galicia, Asturias and the Cantabrian Mountains, the numbers are slowly growing under protection. However, there is strong opposition to wolves being reintroduced into the Alcornocales National Park in Andalusia, southern Spain. In Morocco, wolves survive in the Rif Mountains,[8] and there were only four human deaths attributed to wolves in this area between 1950 and 2000.[9]

The attendant cost of reintroducing wolves into Ireland would also be prohibitive, running to some several million euros at least, with no guarantee of success. Currently, many countries that have protected wolf populations have compensation schemes in place for farm animal losses, including Croatia, France, Italy, Norway, Poland, Portugal, Romania, Spain and the USA. It is also possible to take out an insurance policy in some countries for these losses.[10]

One of the suggested reasons for reintroducing wolves is to control deer numbers, which are rising fast in many countries including Scotland and Ireland. However, US estimates suggest that a wolf kills about eighteen deer annually. A pack of eight wolves might kill 140 deer per year, but their territory could contain more than 4,500 deer.[11] So, the impact of a small number of packs would be limited on overall deer numbers. Although Ireland has a rapidly rising deer population, the reintroduction of wolves would have only a very limited impact of their numbers. Recent work in Scotland suggests that wolves have an impact on more than just deer numbers – they also modify their behaviour and the landscape they inhabit.[12]

The difficulty of maintaining even a small wolf population is illustrated by the experience of Norway, where the hunting (for their skins) of five wolves or 25 per cent of the overall wolf population was authorized, as long as hunting was outside the wolf protection zone. Three-hundred-and-thirty-five hunting licences were granted. Unfortunately, two of the three breeding females were among the five killed, even though they were wearing radio transmitters. This followed a similar cull in 2001 when eight of the twenty-five wolves in the country were legally killed using hunters in helicopters. The comment of the government of Norway is illustrative of the mindset regarding wolves – it claimed that trophy-hunting was the best way to get local people interested in wolves.[13] A similar situation has just occurred in Sweden, where the first wolf cull for forty-five years has taken place, resulting in a major rift between urban and rural attitudes on wolves.[14] It is estimated that between 25 and 50 per cent of a wolf population needs to be culled every year just to maintain population numbers at the same level.[15] So, if wolves were reintroduced into Ireland, it would not be long before organized culls would have to take place to control the numbers.

This brief discussion should highlight two fundamental global issues of conservation. Firstly, how do humans manage and learn to live with large predators?[16] Secondly, what can be done about the ongoing extinction of the world's megafauna (and other species), many of whom are predators.[17]

WOLF TOURISM

There is a growing business in wolf tourism, between exclusively wolf-orientated excursions and trips to broader regions with other large mammals and predators. One of these areas is the Abruzzo region in Italy, which has wolves along with other species including brown bears, golden eagles and chamois antelope–goat.[18] Wildlife tours to countries such as Romania, Sweden, Poland, Spain and Finland focus on large predators, including wolves.[19] There is also a new wolf sanctuary near Nice in France.[20]

Even in Ireland, some wolf tourism occurs, but only to wolves in captivity. An example is the wolf pack in Dublin Zoo, while the Hidden Valley Pet Farm in Kilgarvan, Co. Kerry, has a 'timber wolf' and an 'Arctic wolf' in a wolf enclosure. Both are recognized sub-species of the grey wolf (*Canis lupus*).[21]

THE THREAT FROM PRIVATELY HELD WOLVES AND WOLF/DOG HYBRIDS IN IRELAND

Despite the ferocious reputation of wolves and most people's fear of them, some wolves and possibly wolf-cross/hybrid dogs are being kept in private collections in Ireland. This has emerged as a result of three incidents: one in Fermanagh in 1995; one in Tyrone in 2009; and one in Wexford in 2001 (see below). It has also been revealed that wolf cubs can be bought legally in Ireland and are available from at least one breeding farm. It is very unlikely, however, they are even close to being 100 per cent wolf.

In April 2001, two wolves escaped from a pen in the rear garden of a house in Ballylarkin, Inch, Co. Wexford. They went on to kill the neighbour's pet dog and remained on the loose for over two hours, terrifying the elderly lady who had lost her dog. They were eventually put down by the local vet. The comment of the owner shows a remarkable lack of insight into his so-called pets and the incident that occurred: he said that the attack was most unusual as his wolves were normally placid and would usually shy away from people.[22] In this case, it is most likely that the wolves were behaving territorially. In the wild, they will kill all competing predators in their area, including wolves from other packs. In the Fermanagh and Tyrone cases, the wolves escaped from private owners. The Fermanagh wolf was eventually shot at Lisnaskea.

Remarkably, an academic from the USA who spent several years lecturing in University College Cork, admits that he brought his wolf called *Brenin* into Ireland and that the wolf went out with him on a daily basis and roamed around the countryside.[23] The local people and farmers were clearly oblivious to the fact that this was a wolf and not a domestic dog, despite *Brenin*'s size.

In America, there have been numerous cases of wolves kept as pets and wolf/dog hybrids turning on and attacking their owners and their children and other humans and also pet animals that have come into contact with them. These attacks have resulted in a number of fatalities, particularly the children of the owners and also other children in the neighbourhood. Two examples suffice to illustrate the severe threat that they pose: in one case, a two-year-old boy had his arm ripped off by the family's own 'pet' wolves in Los Angeles, California; while in 1986 in Anchorage, Alaska, a two-year-old girl was killed by a chained wolf hybrid. One website covers the period from 1981 to 1996 and, while by no means comprehensive, lists thirteen fatal attacks on children aged from three months to twelve years, and also twenty-nine children who suffered serious injuries, including severe lacerations resulting in permanent disfigurement, organ damage and loss of limbs.[24] In Bangor, Co. Down, a young girl was injured by a privately owned wolf in 1999 and this prompted a review of legislation concerning the breeding and keeping of wolves and wolf/dog hybrids in Britain and Northern Ireland the following year. Up until this point, there was no legislation governing the keeping of wolves in Britain or Ireland.[25] Domestic dogs, especially the larger varieties, which were bred for fighting, have also been responsible for numerous deaths and injuries and should be treated with the same level of caution. Even small domestic dogs in packs can cause significant sheep losses and this occurs every year in Ireland.

Both these Irish and other attack cases highlight a very serious confusion that exists, with people preferring to possess wild animals than domesticated ones. Wild animals by their very nature will behave as instinct determines, even though individuals may appear tame and comfortable in the presence of humans and in a human environment. It only takes a certain trigger for them to react instinctively. Many people mistakenly believe that because the individual wild animal appears tame they are the same as domesticated animals and can be trusted as such. This is nonsense, as domesticated animals have had the undesirable characteristics (undesirable in a human context) bred out of them over numerous generations, whereas a 'tame' wild animal retains all its normal characteristics and behaviour, whether exhibited or not. Just because wolves look like domestic dogs does not make them any less dangerous.

FUTURE RESEARCH ON IRISH WOLVES

If after reading this book you think I have exhausted all possibilities of finding further information on wolves in Ireland then I am afraid that is not the case. There is easily a lifetime of work that could still be done on the topic and this would include further work on the thousands of historical books and documents now available online or in databases, which were not available in this format when I first started accumulating wolf information, on place-names, the lives of Irish saints, folklore research, literary references, the Bristol custom books and the murage charters for all of the Irish cities and towns to name but a few. Some of this work needs to be carried out by specialists, especially in relation to place-names and folklore.

I intend to carry on with the wolf research. It is in my blood now anyway, so any additional information the reader could provide would be most gratefully received and acknowledged in any future research, publications and editions of this book.

Notes

CHAPTER I. INTRODUCTION

1 J.E. Harting, *British animals extinct within historic times* (London, 1880); J. Fairley, *Irish wild mammals: a guide to the literature* (Galway, 1972; 2nd ed., Galway, 1992); J. Fairley, 'Exports of wild mammal skins from Ireland in the eighteenth century', *Irish Naturalists' Journal*, 21:2 (1983), 75–9; J. Fairley, *An Irish beast book: a natural history of Ireland's furred wildlife* (2nd ed., Belfast, 1984); J. Fairley, *A basket of weasels: the weasel family in Ireland and other furred Irish beasts: bats, the rabbit, hares and some rodents* (Belfast, 2001).
2 J. Waddell, *The prehistoric archaeology of Ireland* (Galway, 1998).
3 S. Buczacki, *Fauna Britannica* (London, 2002).
4 W.E.H. Lecky, *A history of Ireland in the 18th century*, vol. 1 (new ed., London, 1892).
5 Automobile Association, *Book of the British countryside* (2nd rev. version of 1st ed., Basingstoke, 1974).
6 D. Yalden & P. Barrett, *The history of British mammals* (London, 1999); Buczacki, *Fauna Britannica*.
7 P. Capella, 'Swiss afraid of the big, bad wolf', *Guardian*, 2 Feb. 1999.
8 S. Wavell, 'Tooth and claw', *Sunday Times travel supplement*, 8 Aug. 1999.
9 D.H. Chadwick, 'Wolf wars', *National Geographic*, 217:3 (2010), 34–55.
10 D. Attenborough, *The life of mammals* (London, 2002).
11 R.H. Busch, *The wolf almanac* (rev. ed., New York, 1998).
12 P. Whitfield (ed.), *The Marshall illustrated encyclopedia of animals* (London, 1998).
13 S. Williams, 'Wolves on high', *BBC Wildlife Magazine* (July 2004), 30–5.
14 J. Bryner, 'Africa's lone wolf: new species found in Ethopia' (2011) at www.msnbc.msn.com/id/41315587/ns/technology_and_science-science/, accessed 11 Apr. 2011.
15 Busch, *Wolf almanac*.
16 P. Zuppiroli & L. Donnez, 'The Mexican wolf', *Wolf Print*, 22 (2005), 16–19.
17 T. Flannery & P. Schouten, *A gap in nature: discovering the world's extinct animals* (London, 2001).
18 World Conservation Monitoring Centre, *Endangered mammals!* (Chicago, 1995).
19 J. Smyth, 'Climate change linked to floods and heatwaves', *Irish Times*, 29 Nov. 2005.
20 Whitfield, *Marshall illustrated encyclopedia*.
21 World Conservation Monitoring Centre, *Endangered mammals!*
22 Busch, *Wolf almanac*.
23 Whitfield, *Marshall illustrated encyclopedia*.
24 Attenborough, *The life of mammals*.
25 Ibid.

CHAPTER 2. ARCHAEOLOGICAL EVIDENCE

1 P. Sleeman, 'Mammals and mammology' in J.W. Foster & H.C.G. Chesney (eds), *Nature in Ireland: a scientific and cultural history* (Dublin, 1997), pp 241–61.

2 L.H. van Wijngaarden-Bakker, 'Littletonian faunas' in K.J. Edwards & W. Warren (eds), *The quaternary history of Ireland* (London, 1985), pp 233–49.

3 M. Viney, *Ireland: a Smithsonian natural history* (Belfast, 2003).

4 A. Leith Adams, 'Report on the exploration of Shandon Cave', *Transactions of the Royal Irish Academy*, 26 (1876), 187–230; A. Leith Adams, 'Explorations in the Bone Cave of Ballinamintra', *Transactions of the Royal Dublin Society*, 7:2 (1881), 177–266.

5 P. Woodman, M. McCarthy & N. Monaghan, 'The Irish quaternary fauna project', *Quaternary Science Reviews*, 2 (1997), 29–59.

6 A.J. Stuart & L.H. van Wijngaarden-Bakker, 'Quaternary vertebrates' in Edwards & Warren (eds), *The quaternary history of Ireland* (1985), pp 221–33; T. Carruthers, *Kerry: a natural history* (Cork, 1998).

7 Woodman, McCarthy & Monaghan, 'Quaternary fauna project', 129–59.

8 J.C. Coleman & A.W. Stelfox, 'Excavation at Carrigtwohill Caves, Co. Cork', *Irish Naturalists' Journal*, 8:8 (1945), 299–302.

9 R.F. Scharff, H.J. Seymour & E.T. Newton, 'Exploration of Castlepook Cave, Co. Cork', *Proceedings of the Royal Irish Academy*, 34B (1918), 33–72; R.F. Scharff, 'The wolf in Ireland', *Irish Naturalist*, 31:12 (1922), 133–6; H.E. Forrest, 'Prehistoric mammals of Ireland: II', *Irish Naturalists' Journal*, 1:8 (1926), 152–3.

10 R.F. Scharff, R.J. Ussher, G.A.J. Cole, E.T. Newton, A.F. Dixon & T.J. Westropp, 'The exploration of the caves of Co. Clare: being the second report from the committee appointed to explore Irish caves', *Transactions of Royal Irish Academy*, 33B1 (1906), 1–76.

11 P. Nolan, pers. comm.

12 Waddell, *Prehistoric archaeology of Ireland*.

13 Scharff, 'The wolf in Ireland', 133–6.

14 Stuart & van Wijngaarden-Bakker, 'Quaternary vertebrates', pp 221–33.

15 Viney, *Ireland: a Smithsonian natural history*.

16 D. Cabot, *Ireland: a natural history* (London, 1999); R. Lloyd Praeger, *The way that I went: in Irishman in Ireland* (50th anniversary reissue, Cork, 1997); Woodman, McCarthy & Monaghan, 'Quaternary fauna project', 129–59.

17 J. Feehan, 'The heritage of the rocks' in Foster & Chesney (eds), *Nature in Ireland* (1997), pp 3–22.

18 Stuart & van Wijngaarden-Bakker, 'Quaternary vertebrates', pp 221–33.

19 F. Kelly, *Early Irish farming: a study based mainly on the law-texts of the 7th and 8th centuries AD* (Dublin, 1997).

20 Lloyd Praeger, *The way that I went*.

21 D. Hickie, *Native trees and forests of Ireland* (Dublin, 2002).

22 L.H. van Wijngaarden-Bakker, 'Faunal remains and the Irish Mesolithic' in C. Bonesll (ed.), *The Mesolithic in Europe* (Edinburgh, 1989), pp 125–33.

23 Kelly, *Early Irish farming*.

24 Sleeman, 'Mammals and mammology', pp 241–61.

25 Scharff, 'The wolf in Ireland', 133–6.

26 Waddell, *Prehistoric archaeology of Ireland*.

27 A.H. Davison, J. Orr, A.W. Stelfox & J.A.A. Stendall, 'Excavations of White Park Bay kitchen midden site', *Irish Naturalists' Journal*, 1:14 (1927), 280–2, 284.

28 F. Mitchell & M. Ryan, *Reading the Irish landscape* (3rd ed., Dublin, 2001).

29 B. Raftery, *Pagan Celtic Ireland: the enigma of the Irish Iron Age* (London, 1994).

30 Woodman, McCarthy & Monaghan, 'Quaternary fauna project', 129–59.

31 M. Dowd, 'Glencurran Cave, Tullycommon, Co. Clare' online at www.excavations.ie/Pages/Details.php?Year =&County=Clare&id=11108, accessed 1 July 2011.

32 van Wijngaarden-Bakker, 'Littletonian faunas', pp 233–49; Waddell, *Prehistoric archaeology of Ireland*.

33 Stuart & van Wijngaarden-Bakker, 'Quaternary vertebrates', pp 221–33.

34 C. Newman, 'Ballinderry crannóg no. 2, Co. Offaly: pre-crannóg early medieval horizon', *Journal of Irish Archaeology*, 11 (2002), 99–123.

35 J.T. Lang, 'Viking Age decorated wood: a study of its ornament and style', *Medieval Dublin excavations, 1962–1981* B1 (1988).

36 Cabot, *Ireland: a natural history*; Scharff, 'The wolf in Ireland', 133–6; W. Thompson, *Natural history of Ireland*, ix: *mammalia, reptiles and fishes also invertebrata* (London, 1856). A recent dating study of mostly Ulster ringforts suggest a date of between AD500 and 900: M. Stout, *The Irish ringfort* (Dublin, 1997).

37 Lloyd Praeger, *The way that I went*.

38 J. Fairley, *An Irish beast book: a natural history of Ireland's furred wildlife* (2nd ed., Belfast, 1984).

39 Viney, *Ireland: a Smithsonian natural history*.

40 F.A. Allen, 'The wolf in Scotland and Ireland', *Transactions of the Caradoc and Severn Valley Field Club*, 5 (1909), 68–74.

41 H.H. Lamb, *Climate history and the modern world* (2nd ed., London, 1985). The information on the use of the fence was based on surviving contemporary records.

42 C. Smith, *Ancient and present state of the county of Kerry* (Dublin, 1756).

43 R. Lloyd Praeger, *Natural history of Ireland: a sketch of its flora and fauna* (London, 1950).

44 E. MacLysaght, *Irish life in the seventeenth century* (4th ed., Dublin, 1979).

45 Scharff, 'The wolf in Ireland', 133–6; MacLysaght, *Irish life in the seventeenth century*, 4th ed.

46 Sleeman, 'Mammals and mammology', pp 241–61.

47 M.J. Higgins, 'Wolves and foxes in Irish folklore' (BA dissertation, NUIG, 2007).

48 Kelly, *Early Irish farming*.

CHAPTER 3. NAMES

1 J.E. Harting, *British animals extinct within historic times* (London, 1880).

2 D. Cabot, *Ireland: a natural history* (London, 1999); P.W. Joyce, *A smaller social history of ancient Ireland* (London, 1908); S. Ó Súilleabháin, *A handbook of Irish folklore* (Detroit, 1970); F. Kelly, *Early Irish farming: a study based mainly on the law-texts of the 7th and 8th centuries AD* (Dublin, 1997).

3 P.W. Joyce, *The origin and history of Irish names of places*, 2 vols (1891, 1995); Cabot, *Ireland: a natural history*.

4 Ó Súilleabháin, *Handbook of Irish folklore*; Joyce, *Origin and history*; Kelly, *Early Irish farming*; Cabot, *Ireland: a natural history*.

5 R.F. Scharff, 'The wolf in Ireland', *The Irish Naturalist*, 31:12 (1922), 133–6; Kelly, *Early Irish farming*.

6 Scharff, 'The wolf in Ireland', 133–6; Ó Súilleabháin, *Handbook of Irish folklore*; D. McManus, *A guide to ogham* (Maynooth, 1991).

7 F. Ó Riain, 'Where's that: Bunratty 1425', *Irish Times*, 2 Dec. 2002.

8 Scharff, 'The wolf in Ireland', 133–6.

9 Her Majesty's Stationery Office, *Census of Ireland: general alphabetical Index to the townlands and towns, parishes and baronies of Ireland* (Dublin, 1861).

10 C. Ó Crualaoich, pers. comm.

11 Joyce, *Origin and history*.

12 P. Nolan, 'The wolves of Co. Clare', *The Other Clare*, 28 (2004), 63–8.

13 Joyce, *Origin and history*.

14 C. Ó Crualaoich, pers. comm.

15 N. Mac Coitir, *Ireland's animals: myths, legends and folklore* (Cork, 2010).

16 Joyce, *Origin and history*. This comes from a gloss in the Féilire of Aengus.

17 D. Flanagan & L. Flanagan, *Irish place-names* (Dublin, 1994).

18 www.logainm.ie.

19 www.placenamesni.org.

20 Mac Coitir, *Ireland's animals*.

21 C. Ó Crualaoich, pers. comm.

22 J.P. O'Reilly, 'On the waste of the coast of Ireland as a factor in Irish history', *Proceedings of the Royal Irish Academy*, 24B2 (1902), 95–202.

23 Joyce, *Origin and history*.

24 C. Ó Crualaoich, pers. comm.

25 C. Carson, *The Táin: a new translation of the* Táin Bó Cúailnge (London, 2007).

26 T. Tynan, 'Ancient Christian burial at Wolfhill, Kilfeacle, Co. Leix', *Journal of the Royal Society of Antiquaries of Ireland*, 62 (1932), 119–20; Anon., 'My, what big teeth you have', *Easyjet inflight magazine* (Mar. 2005).

27 M. Maher, pers. comm.

28 T. Lyng, *Castlecomer connections* (Castlecomer, Co. Kilkenny, 1984).

29 M. O'Dowd, 'Calendar of state papers, Ireland, Tudor period, 1571–1575' (London, 2000).

30 C. Aybes & D.W. Yalden, 'Place-name evidence for the former distribution of wolves and beavers in Britain', *Mammal Review*, 25:4 (2008), 201–26.

31 L. Flanagan, 'An index to minor place-names from the 6-inch Ordnance Survey: Co. Derry', *Bulletin of the Ulster Place-name Society* 2:2 (1979), 61–74.

32 L. Flanagan, 'An index to minor place-names from the 6-inch Ordnance Survey: Co. Armagh', *Bulletin of the Ulster Place-name Society* 2:4 (1981–2), 76–84.

33 R. Lloyd Praeger, 'Botanizing in the Ards', *The Irish Naturalist*, 12:2 (1903), 254–65.

34 P. Duffy, *Landscapes of south Ulster: a parish atlas of the diocese of Clogher* (Belfast, 1993).

35 S. O'Boyle, *Ogham: the poets' secret* (Dublin, 1980).

36 J. Rhys, 'The ogham-inscribed stones in the collection of the Royal Irish Academy', *Journal of the Royal Society of Antiquaries of Ireland*, 32 (1902), 1–43; C. Swift, *Ogham stones and the earliest Irish Christians* (Maynooth, 1997); S. Connolly & A. Moroney, *Ogham: ancestors remembered in stone* (Drogheda, 2000).

37 McManus, *Guide to ogham*.

38 O'Boyle, *Ogham*.

39 Connolly & Moroney, *Ogham*.

40 McManus, *Guide to ogham*.

41 McManus, *Guide to ogham*.

42 B. McWilliams, *Weather eye: the final year* (Dublin, 2009).

43 www.daire.org 2005, www.daire.org/names/celticirishmale.html, www.daire.org/names/celticirishfem.html, www.daire.org/names/celticirishsurs.html.

44 R.E Matheson, *Special report on surnames in Ireland, 1890* (Dublin, 1894).

45 www.goireland.com/genealogy/family.htm?familyid=314, Woulfe surname.

46 T.J. Westropp, *Folklore of Clare: a folklore survey of County Clare and County Clare folk tales and myths* (Ennis 2000), p. 62 n. 2.

47 http://www.mactireofskye.webs.com/ (accessed 1 July 2011).

48 C. Ó Crualaoich, pers. comm.

49 S. de Bhulb, *Sloinnte uile Eireann: all Ireland surnames* (Ireland, 2002).

50 A.K. Longfield, *Anglo-Irish trade in the sixteenth century* (London, 1929).

51 B. Bourke, *Rabbiting on, school and parish: Breaffy, 1898–1990* (Sligo, 1990), p. 129.

52 R.L. Grambo & D.J. Cox, *Wolf: legend, enemy, icon* (London, 2005).

53 A. Crossly, *The significance of most things that are born in heraldry with the explanation of their natural qualities* (Dublin, 1724).

54 J. Fairley, *An Irish beast book: a natural history of Ireland's furred wildlife* (2nd ed., Belfast, 1984).

CHAPTER 4. MYTHOLOGY, FOLKLORE AND SUPERSTITIONS

1 S. Ó Súilleabháin, *A handbook of Irish folklore* (Detroit, 1970).
2 D. Pickering, *Dictionary of superstitions* (London, 1998).
3 R.L.Grambo & D.J. Cox, *Wolf: legend, enemy, icon* (London, 2005).
4 Pickering, *Dictionary of superstitions.*
5 Grambo & Cox, *Wolf: legend, enemy, icon.*
6 Ibid.
7 J. Dunne, 'Folklore no.1: the Fenian traditions of Sliabh-Na-M-Ban', *Transactions of the Kilkenny Archaeological Society*, 1:3 (1851), 333–62.
8 S. O'Sullivan (ed.), *Folktales of Ireland* (London, 1966).
9 Ibid.
10 J. Fairley, *An Irish beast book: a natural history of Ireland's furred wildlife* (2nd ed., Belfast, 1984).
11 D. Toomey, pers. comm.
12 C. Carson, *The Táin: a new translation of the* Táin Bó Cúailnge (London, 2007).
13 G. Cunningham & R. Coghlan, *The mystery animals of Ireland* (Bideford, 2010).
14 N. Mac Coitir, *Ireland's animals: myths, legends and folklore* (Cork, 2010).
15 C.W. Eliot, *Epic and saga* (Montana, 2003).
16 M. O'Daly (ed.), *The heroic biography of Cormac mac Airt, Cath Maige Mucrama: the battle of Mag Mucrama* (Dublin, 1975).
17 Mac Coitir, *Ireland's animals.*
18 Grambo & Cox, *Wolf: legend, enemy, icon.*
19 Ibid.
20 M. Aldhouse-Green, *Celtic art: reading the messages* (London, 1996).
21 Ibid.
22 F. Kelly, *Early Irish farming: a study based mainly on the law-texts of the 7th and 8th centuries AD* (Dublin, 1997).
23 M. Viney, *Ireland: a Smithsonian natural history* (Belfast, 2003).
24 J. Waddell, 'Rathcroghan: a royal site in Connacht', *Journal of Irish Archaeology*, 1 (1983), 21–46.
25 Mac Coitir, *Ireland's animals.*
26 P.W. Joyce (1891) *The origin and history of Irish names of places*, 2 vols (Dublin, 1891, repr. 1995).
27 R. O'Flaherty, *A chorographical description of West or H-Iar Connaught*, ed. J. Hardiman (1684; Dublin, 1846).
28 C. Kenny, *Molaise: abbot of Leighlin and hermit of Holy Island* (Killala, 1998).
29 G. Cambrensis, *Topographia Hibernia or the history and topography of Ireland*, trans. J.J. O'Meara (Portlaoise, revised ed., 1982).
30 Ibid.
31 Kelly, *Early Irish farming.*
32 Ibid.
33 Grambo & Cox, *Wolf: legend, enemy, icon.*
34 D. Moore, *The accidental pilgrim: travels with a Celtic saint* (Dublin, 2004).
35 A. Cahill, 'The wolf-men of Ossory', *Ireland's Own*, 4,685 (1999), 12.
36 Ibid.
37 Ibid.
38 C. Plummer, *Vitae sanctorum Hibernia*, 1 (Oxford, 1910).
39 M. Belozerskaya, *The Medici giraffe and other tales of exotic animals and power* (New York, 2006).
40 Kelly, *Early Irish farming.*
41 R. Lloyd Praeger, *Natural history of Ireland: a sketch of its flora and fauna* (London, 1950).

42 Kelly, *Early Irish farming*.

43 Ibid.

44 Ibid.

45 F.A. Allen, 'The wolf in Scotland and Ireland', *Transactions of the Caradoc and Severn Valley field club*, 5 (1909), 68–74.

46 J.E. Harting, *British animals extinct within historic times* (London, 1880).

47 Grambo & Cox, *Wolf: legend, enemy, icon*.

48 Kelly, *Early Irish farming*.

49 Ibid.

50 K. Thomas, *Man and the natural world: changing attitudes in England, 1500–1800* (London, 1984).

51 Anon., 'Co. Kildare in 1683', TCD MS 1.1.2 (1683).

52 L. Echard, *An exact description of Ireland* (London, 1691).

53 G. Miege, *The present state of Great Britain and Ireland in three parts ... containing an accurate and impartial account of these great and famous islands, of their several counties and their inhabitants ... of the vast, populous and opulent city of London ... of the Britains original, language, temper, genius, religion, morals, trade ... with the lists of the present officers in church and state ... to which are added, maps of the three kingdoms, also the present state of His Majesty's dominions in Germany ... and a new map of them all* (London, 1707); D. Ó Hógáin, *Irish superstitions* (Dublin, 1995); S.J. Maguire, 'Some notes on the natural history of Iar-Connacht in the seventeenth century', *Galway Reader*, 4:2/3 (1954), 102–6; J. Hardiman, *The history of the town and county of the town of Galway* (Dublin, 1820).

54 C. Hole (ed.), *The encyclopedia of superstitions* (Oxford, 1980).

55 J. Grub, 'The wolf-days of Ireland', *Zoologist*, 20 (1862), 7996–7.

56 Cahill, 'The wolf-men of Ossory', 12.

57 Fairley, *Irish beast book*.

58 J.D. O'Dowd, 'Stories about wolves', *Béaloideas*, 10 (1940), 287–9.

59 Fairley, *Irish beast book*.

60 M.J. Higgins, 'Wolves and foxes in Irish folklore' (BA dissertation, NUIG, 2007).

61 Ibid.

62 Cunningham & Coghlan, *Mystery animals of Ireland*.

63 Ibid.

64 W. Gaynor, pers. comm.

65 W. Gaynor, pers. comm.

66 S. Buczacki, *Fauna Britannica* (London, 2002).

67 S. Young, *AD500: a journey through the dark isles of Britain and Ireland* (London, 2005).

68 K.H. Jackson, *A Celtic miscellany: translations from the Celtic literature* (London, 1951); D. Green & F. O'Connor (eds), *A golden treasury of Irish poetry, AD600 to 1200* (London, 1967); Kelly, *Early Irish farming*.

69 Mac Coitir, *Ireland's animals*.

70 Fynes Moryson, *An itinerary: containing his ten years travel through the twelve dominions of Germany, Bohemia, Switzerland, Netherland, Denmark, Poland, Italy, Turkey, France, England, Scotland and Ireland*, 3 vols (1617; London, 1735), ii (*History of Ireland, 1599–1603, with a short narrative of the state of the kingdom from 1169*).

71 A. Bourke et al. (eds), *The Field Day anthology of Irish writing, IV & V: women's writing and traditions* (Cork, 2002). In the second stanza, the second line of the refrain is slightly different: 'The great grey wolf with scraping claws, lest he' (E. McCracken, *The Irish woods since Tudor times: distribution and exploitation* (Newton Abbott, 1971)).

72 Cabot, *Ireland: a natural history*.

73 H. Savile & A. Marwell, *Advice to a painter: being a satyr upon the French king, Admiral Tourvill, Irish camp at Havre de Grace, murmuring, jacobites &c* (1692); Harting, *British animals*.

74 Allen, 'The wolf in Scotland and Ireland'.
75 Harting, *British animals*; Fairley, *Irish beast book*.
76 Buczacki, *Fauna Britannica*.
77 J. Derrick, 'Image of Ireland', *Lord Somer's Tracts*, 1 (1581), 579.
78 V. di Martino, *Roman Ireland* (Cork, 2003).
79 S. Heaney, *Wintering out* (London, 1972).
80 J. K'eogh, *Zoologia medicinalis Hibernica* (Dublin, 1739).
81 Ibid.
82 Lady Wilde, *Irish cures, mystic charms and superstitions* (New York, 1991).
83 Pickering, *Dictionary of superstitions*.
84 Ibid.
85 Ibid.
86 Grambo & Cox, *Wolf*.
87 B. Schott, *Schott's food and drink miscellany* (London, 2003).
88 Young, *AD500*.
89 J. Speede, *The theatre of the empire of Great Britaine* (London, 1612)
90 W. Camden, *Britannia* (1586, Newton Abbott, facsimile ed. 1971).
91 Allen, 'The wolf in Scotland and Ireland', 68–74.
92 D. Toomey, pers. comm., 2009.
93 Grambo & Cox, *Wolf: legend, enemy, icon*.
94 P. Simons, *Weird weather* (London, 1996).
95 Allen, 'The wolf in Scotland and Ireland', 68–74.
96 Grambo & Cox, *Wolf: legend, enemy, icon*.
97 Cahill, 'The wolf-men of Ossory', 12.
98 Grambo & Cox, *Wolf: legend, enemy, icon*.
99 Pickering, *Dictionary of superstitions*.
1 Ibid.
2 Cambrensis, *Topographia Hibernia*.
3 Ibid.
4 Cunningham & Coghlan, *Mystery animals of Ireland*.
5 Cahill, 'The wolf-men of Ossory', 12.
6 Ibid.
7 Camden, *Britannia*.
8 P.E. Keck, et al., 'Lycanthropy: alive and well in the twentieth century', *Psychological Medicine*, 18:1 (1988), 113–20.
9 Pickering, *Dictionary of superstitions*.
10 Cambrensis, *Topographia Hibernia*.
11 N.S. Scheinfeld & V. Deleo, 'Photosensitivity in lupus erythematosus', *Photodermatology Photoimmunology Photomedecin*, 20 (2004), 272–9.
12 D. Wendelin, D. Pope & S. Mallory, 'Hypertrichosis', *Journal of the American Academy of Dermatology*, 48:2 (2003), 161–79.
13 J.W. Foster, 'Encountering traditions' in J.W. Foster & H.C.G. Chesney (eds), *Nature in Ireland: a scientific and cultural history* (Dublin, 1997), pp 23–70.
14 C. Hole (ed.), *The Encyclopedia of superstitions* (Oxford, 1980).
15 Grambo & Cox, *Wolf: legend, enemy, icon*.
16 Cahill, 'The wolf-men of Ossory', 12.
17 E. Windisch, *Irische text mit Übersetzungen und Wörterbuch*, 1 (Berlin, 1880).
18 J. Matthews, *Celtic totem animals* (Boston, 2002).
19 Hole, *Encyclopedia of superstitions*.
20 Thomas, *Man and the natural world*.
21 J.W. Foster, 'Nature and nation in the nineteenth century' in Foster & Chesney (eds), *Nature in Ireland* (Dublin, 1997), pp 409–39.

22 Grambo & Cox, *Wolf: legend, enemy, icon*.

23 K. Meyer, *Contributions to Irish lexicography*, I, a–c (London, 1906).

CHAPTER 5. THE HISTORIC RECORD UP TO AD1786 AND BEYOND?

1 P.W. Joyce, *A smaller social history of ancient Ireland* (London, 1908).

2 J. Feehan, 'Threat and conservation: attitudes to nature in Ireland' in Foster & Chesney (eds), *Nature in Ireland*, pp 573–96.

3 S. Young, *AD500: a journey through the dark isles of Britain and Ireland* (London, 2005).

4 J. Fairley, *An Irish beast book: a natural history of Ireland's furred wildlife* (2nd ed., Belfast, 1984).

5 C. Moriarty, 'The early naturalists' in J.W. Foster & H.C.G. Chesney (eds), *Nature in Ireland: a scientific and cultural history* (Dublin, 1997), pp 71–90.

6 D. Cabot, *Ireland: a natural history* (London, 1999).

7 J.H. Todd (ed.), *The Irish version of the* Historia Britonum *of Nennius* (Dublin, 1848); G. Cambrensis, *Topographia Hibernia or the history and topography of Ireland*, trans. J.J. O'Meara (Portlaoise, revised ed. 1982); Fairley, *Irish beast book*.

8 F. Kelly, *Early Irish farming: a study based mainly on the law-texts of the 7th and 8th centuries AD* (Dublin, 1997).

9 A. Cahill, 'The wolf-men of Ossory', *Ireland's Own*, 4:685 (1999), 12.

10 Kelly, *Early Irish farming*.

11 Ibid.

12 Automobile Association, *Book of the British countryside* (2nd ed., Hampshire, 1974).

13 S. Trimmer, *A description of a set of prints of English history: contained in a set of easy lessons* (London, 1792).

14 Cambrensis, *Topographia Hibernia*.

15 E. Curtis, *Calendar of Ormond deeds, 1172–1350* (Dublin, 1932).

16 E.J. Lowe, *Natural phenomena and chronology of the seasons; being an account of remarkable frosts, droughts, thunderstorms, gales, floods, earthquakes etc., also diseases, cattle plagues, famines etc., which have occurred in the British Isles since AD220, chronologically arranged* (London, 1870).

17 Fairley, *An Irish beast book*.

18 E. FitzPatrick, M. O'Brien & P. Walsh (eds), *Archaeological investigations in Galway City, 1987–1998* (Wicklow, 2004).

19 Kelly, *Early Irish farming*; F. McCormick, 'Early evidence for wild animals in Ireland' in N. Benecke (ed.), *The Holocene history of the European vertebrate fauna* (1999), 355–71.

20 H.H. Lamb, *Climate history and the modern world* (2nd ed., London, 1985).

21 P. Simons, *Weird weather* (London, 1996).

22 F. Ludlow, pers. comm.

23 A.K. Longfield, *Anglo-Irish trade in the sixteenth century* (London, 1929). Flavin and Jones show the exact same detail as being for 25 June 1504, and state that the skins were of fox (S. Flavin & E.T. Jones (eds), *Bristol's trade with Ireland and the continent, 1503–1601: the evidence of the exchequer custom accounts* (Dublin, 2009)). Indeed, no wolfskins are listed for the tax year 1503–4, whereas there were plenty of fox skins. In 1504–5, however, Irish vessels carried 295 and English vessels carried 103 wolfskins to Bristol from Ireland, valued at 1½*d.* each (Longfield, *Anglo-Irish trade*). It is possible that Longfield put down all fox skins as wolfskins, as she does not list fox skins in her end table, whereas Flavin and Jones record numerous ships carrying fox skins (Flavin & Jones (eds), *Bristol's trade*). Only a check of the original two volumes from 1503–4 and 1504–5 will resolve this.

24 Flavin & Jones (eds), *Bristol's trade*.
25 Ibid.
26 Longfield, *Anglo-Irish trade*.
27 Flavin & Jones (eds), *Bristol's trade*.
28 Ibid.
29 Ibid.
30 Longfield, *Anglo-Irish trade*.
31 J.W. Foster, 'Encountering traditions' in Foster & Chesney (eds), *Nature in Ireland* (Dublin, 1997), pp 23–70.
32 Feehan, 'Threat and conservation', pp 573–96.
33 F.A. Allen, 'The wolf in Scotland and Ireland', *Transactions of the Caradoc and Severn Valley Field Club*, 5 (1909), 68–74.
34 R.F. Scharff, 'The wolf in Ireland', *Irish Naturalist*, 31:12 (1922), 133–6.
35 Anon., 'Illustrative notes to Sir Henry Sidney's memoir', *Ulster Journal of Archaeology*, 1:3 (1855), 43–52.
36 E. Campion, *A historie of Ireland* (Dublin, 1633, facsimile ed. 1940).
37 G. Turberville, *The noble art of venerie or hunting, wherein is handled and set out the vertues, natures and properties of fifteene sundrie chaces, together with the order and maner how to hunte and kill everyone of them. Translated and collected, for pleasure of all noblemen and gentlemen, out of the best approved authors which have written anything concerning the same, and reduced into such order and proper termes as are used here in the noble realme of Englande* (London, 1575). This is usually found printed with George Turberville's *Bookes of faiilconrie*, to whom, therefore, it has been generally attributed.
38 Allen, 'The wolf in Scotland and Ireland', 68–74.
39 G.B. Corbet & S. Harris (eds), *The handbook of British mammals* (Oxford, 1991).
40 Fairley, *Irish beast book*.
41 M. Viney, *Ireland: a Smithsonian natural history* (Belfast, 2003).
42 Joyce, *A smaller social history*.
43 Allen, 'The wolf in Scotland and Ireland', 68–74.
44 Great Britain Census Office, *Census of Ireland, 1851: supplementary report on tables of deaths* (London, 1852), pp 41–364.
45 N. Hanson, *The confident hope of a miracle: the story of the Spanish Armada* (London, 2005).
46 Fairley, *Irish beast book*.
47 Allen, 'The wolf in Scotland and Ireland', 68–74; J.S. Brewer & W. Bullen, *Calendar of the Carew manuscripts preserved in the Archiepiscopal Library at Lambeth, 1575–1588* (London, 1868); D. Cabot, *Ireland: a natural history* (London, 1999).
48 C. Falls, *Elizabeth's Irish wars* (London, repr. ed. 1996).
49 Ibid.
50 E. MacLysaght, *Irish life in the seventeenth century* (2nd ed., Cork, 1950).
51 Lewis, *Hunting in Ireland*.
52 Fynes Moryson, *An itinerary: containing his ten years travel through the twelve dominions of Germany, Bohemia, Switzerland, Netherland, Denmark, Poland, Italy, Turkey, France, England, Scotland and Ireland*, 3 vols (1617; London, 1735), ii (*History of Ireland, 1599–1603, with a short narrative of the state of the kingdom from 1169*).
53 Ibid.
54 P. O'Sullivan Beare, *Historiae Catholicae Iberniae compendium excusum a Petro Crasbeeckio, Ulyssippone*, ed. Matthew Kelly (1621; Dublin, 1850).
55 G. Bennett, *History of Bandon* (Cork, 1869); E. McCracken, *The Irish woods since Tudor times: distribution and exploitation* (Newton Abbott, 1971).
56 Fairley, *Irish beast book*.
57 M. Viney, *Ireland: a Smithsonian natural history* (Belfast, 2003).
58 McCracken, *The Irish woods*.

59 T. Blennerhassett, 'A direction for the plantation of Ulster, containing in it six principal things', MS (1610).
60 Brewer & Bullen, *Calendar of the Carew manuscripts*.
61 Scharff, 'The wolf in Ireland', 133–6.
62 Lewis, *Hunting in Ireland*.
63 D. Coombs, *Sport and the countryside in the English paintings, watercolours and prints* (New York, 1978).
64 E.D. Borrowes-Bart, 'The French settlers in Ireland, no. 6, The Huguenot colony at Portarlington, in the Queen's County, continued', *UJA*, 1st ser., 3 (1855), 213–19.
65 Fairley, *Irish beast book*.
66 P.W. Joyce, *The origin and history of Irish names of places*, 2 vols (Dublin, facsimile repr. 1995); Foster, 'Encountering traditions', pp 23–70; R. O'Flaherty, *A chorographical description of west or H-Iar Connaught*, ed. J. Hardiman (1684; Dublin, 1846).
67 Cahill, 'The wolf-men of Ossory', 12.
68 Fairley, *Irish beast book*.
69 'Declaration of the lord lieutenant of Ireland (Cromwell) in answer to the declaration of the Irish prelates and clergy in a conventicle of Clonmacnoise, at the Old Bayley, 21 March 1650': J.P. Prendergast, *The Cromwellian settlement of Ireland* (3rd ed., Dublin, 1922).
70 Prendergast, *Cromwellian settlement*.
71 J.E. Harting, *British animals extinct within historic times* (London, 1880); Prendergast, *Cromwellian settlement*.
72 S.J. Maguire, 'Some notes on the natural history of Iar-Connacht in the seventeenth century', *Galway Reader*, 4:2/3 (1954), 102–6.
73 V. Ball, 'Records of the export of Irish wolf-dogs to the east in the 17th century', *Irish Naturalist*, 3:5 (1894), 101–2; Allen, 'The wolf in Scotland and Ireland', 68–74.
74 Scharff, 'Wolf in Ireland', 133–6.
75 Ibid.
76 Ibid.
77 R. Dunlop, *Ireland under the Commonwealth* (Manchester, 1913).
78 J. Lacey, *A candle in the window* (Dublin, 1999).
79 E. MacLysaght, *Irish life in the seventeenth century* (4th ed., Dublin, 1979).
80 MacLysaght, *Irish life in the seventeenth century*, 4th ed.
81 Maguire, 'Some notes on the natural history of Iar-Connacht', 102–6.
82 J.E. Doherty & D.J. Hickey, *A chronology of Irish history since 1500* (Dublin, 1989).
83 Prendergast, *Cromwellian settlement*.
84 Ibid.
85 Maguire, 'Some notes on the natural history of Iar-Connacht', 102–6.
86 Ibid.
87 R. Lydekker (ed.), *The royal natural history*, 1 (London, 1894).
88 Lewis, *Hunting in Ireland*.
89 E.A. D'Alton, *History of Ireland: from the earliest times to the present day*, half-vol. 4: *1649 to 1782* (London, 1920).
90 McCracken, *The Irish woods*.
91 MacLysaght, *Irish life in the seventeenth century*, 2nd ed.
92 F. Ó Riain, 'Where's that: Ballymorgan 1453', *Irish Times*, 20 June 2003; Prendergast, *Cromwellian settlement*.
93 R.L. Grambo & D.J. Cox, *Wolf: legend, enemy, icon* (London, 2005).
94 Ibid.
95 R.P. Mahaffy (ed.), *Calendar of the state papers relating to Ireland preserved in the Public Record Office, 1647–1660* (London, 1903).
96 R.P. Mahaffy (ed.), *Calendar of the state papers relating to Ireland preserved in the Public Record Office, 1663–1665* (London, 1907).

97 R.P. Mahaffy (ed.), *Calendar of the state papers relating to Ireland preserved in the Public Record Office, 1663–1665* (London, 1907).

98 Prendergast, *Cromwellian settlement*; T. Herbert, 'The wolves in Ireland', *Zoologist*, 3:9 (1885), 268. See also C. Archibald & J. Bell, 'Wolves in Ireland', *Ulster Journal of Archaeology*, 2:1(1854), 281.

99 McCracken, *Irish woods*.

 1 G.N. Nuttall-Smith, *The chronicles of a Puritan family in Ireland* (Oxford, 1923).

 2 W. Thompson, *Natural history of Ireland*, iv: *mammalia, reptiles and fishes also invertebrata* (London, 1856).

 3 Endorsed at Dublin Castle, 29 Apr. 1663. See J.G.A. Prim, 'Petition from William Collowe to the Duke of Ormond dated 29 Apr. 1663, for permission to kill wolves', *Journal of the Kilkenny and South-east of Ireland Archaeological Society*, new ser., 6 (1867), 211–12.

 4 C. Croaffts, 'Wolves, two letters from Christopher Croaffts to Sir John Perceval', Egmont Manuscripts, *Historic Manuscripts Commission report*, 2 (1909), p. 5.

 5 Fairley, *Irish beast book*.

 6 Lewis, *Hunting in Ireland*.

 7 Lord Broghill, 'Two letters from Lord Broghill to the earl of Dorset', De La Warr Manuscript, *Historic Manuscripts Commission report*, no. 4 (1874), p. 280.

 8 Richard Caulfield, *Youghal Corporation council book from 1610 to 1659, from 1666 to 1687 and from 1690 to 1800* (Youghal, 1878).

 9 MacLysaght, *Irish life in the seventeenth century*; Cabot, *Ireland: a natural history*; Fairley, *Irish beast book*.

10 Cox, *The gentleman's recreation, in four parts: viz. hunting, fowling, hawking, fishing, wherein those generous exercises are largely treated of* (1st ed., London, 1677); Lewis, *Hunting in Ireland*.

11 Anon., 'Co. Kildare in 1683' (TCD MS 1.1.2).

12 O'Flaherty, *Chorographical description of West or H-Iar Connaught*.

13 MacLysaght, *Irish life in the seventeenth century*, 2nd ed.

14 Allen, 'The wolf in Scotland and Ireland', 68–74.

15 Archibald & Bell, 'Wolves in Ireland', 281; Herbert, 'Wolves in Ireland', 268.

16 T.B. Macauley, *History of England from the accession of James I*, 5 vols (Philadelphia, PA, 1848).

17 L. Echard, *An exact description of Ireland* (London, 1691); Miege, *The present state of Great Britain and Ireland* (1707).

18 J. Compton, *A compendious system of chronology* (Belfast, 1823).

19 W. Thompson, *Belfast and its environs with a tour to the Giant's Causeway: containing a map, plan, and numerous illustrations on wood* (Dublin, 1842); McCracken, *Irish woods*.

20 P. Murray, pers. comm.

21 Herbert, 'Wolves in Ireland', 268.

22 MacLysaght, *Irish life in the seventeenth century*, 4th ed.

23 Ibid.

24 Lewis, *Hunting in Ireland*.

25 E.D. Akinson, *An Ulster parish: being a history of Donaghcloney (Waringstown)* (Dublin, 1898); J. O'Donovan, *Ordnance Survey Letters Wicklow: letters relating to the antiquities of County Wicklow containing information collected during progress of the Ordnance Survey in 1838* (Dublin, 1838); Harting, *British animals*; Fairley, *Irish beast book*; McCracken, *Irish woods*; N. Fisher McMillan, 'Last Irish wolves', *Irish Naturalists' Journal*, 17:3 (1971), 103.

26 Cahill, 'The wolf-men of Ossory', 12; Fairley, *Irish beast book*.

27 T.A. Lunham, 'Bishop Dive Downes: visitation of his diocese, 1699–1702', *Journal of the Cork Historical and Archaeological Society*, 15 (1909), 163–80.

28 J. Sinclair, *Statistical account of Scotland*, xii: *North and West Perthshire* (Edinburgh, 1791–9).

29 Joyce, *Origin and history*.

30 Maguire, 'Some notes on the natural history of Iar-Connacht', 102–6; J. Hardiman, *The history of the town and county of the town of Galway* (Dublin, 1820); Scharff, 'The wolf in Ireland', 133–6.
31 M. Maher, pers. comm.
32 Scharff, 'The wolf in Ireland', 133–6; W.E.H. Lecky, *A history of Ireland in the 18th century*, 1 (new ed., London, 1892); McCracken, *Irish woods*.
33 C. Smith, *Ancient and present state of the county of Kerry* (Dublin, 1756).
34 J. O'Donovan (ed.), *Annála ríoghachta Éireann: Annals of the kingdom of Ireland, by the Four Masters, from the earliest period to the year 1616*, 6 vols (Dublin, 1851).
35 C. Hepworth Holland, *The Irish landscape: a scenery to celebrate* (Edinburgh, 2003).
36 C. Mackenzie, *The natural history of all the most remarkable quadrupeds, birds, fishes, reptiles and insects; abridged from Buffon, Goldsmith, Cuvier and other eminent naturalists, with upwards of one hundred beautiful cuts* (London, 1860); O'Donovan, *Ordnance Survey Letters Wicklow*; Harting, *British animals*.
37 M. Jones, 'The man from South Yorkshire who had the privilege of seeing one of the last surviving wolves in the British Isles', *Sorby Record*, 36 (2000), 28–31.
38 O'Donovan (ed.), *Annála ríoghachta Éireann*.
39 J. O'Donovan, *Ordnance Survey Letters Londonderry: letters relating to the antiquities of County Londonderry containing information collected during progress of the Ordnance Survey in 1837* (Dublin, 1834).
40 Maguire, 'Some notes on the natural history of Iar-Connacht', 102–6.
41 A. Edwards, *Edward's Cork remembrancer; or, tablet of memory, enumerating every remarkable circumstance that has happened in the city and county of Cork and in the kingdom at large. Including all the memorable events in Great Britain ... also the remarkable earthquakes, famines ... fires, and all other accidents of moment in every quarter of the globe, from the earliest period, to the 1792* (Cork, 1792).
42 MacLysaght, *Irish life in the seventeenth century*, 4th ed.
43 Herbert, 'Wolves in Ireland', 268.
44 D. O'Driscoll, pers. comm.
45 Fairley, *Irish beast book*; Allen, 'The wolf in Scotland and Ireland', 68–74.
46 W.P. Burke, *The Irish priest in the penal times (1660–1760): from the state papers and HM record office Dublin and London, the Bodleian Library and the British Museum* (Waterford, 1914, repr. 1969).
47 Allen, 'The wolf in Scotland and Ireland', 68–74.
48 Ibid.
49 H.E. Forrest, 'Prehistoric mammals of Ireland: II', *Irish Naturalists' Journal*, 1:8 (1926), 152–3.
50 H.D. Richardson, 'The Irish wolf-dog', *Irish Penny Journal* (1841). See also Lewis, *Hunting in Ireland*.
51 Miege, *Present state of Great Britain and Ireland*; Maguire, 'Some notes on the natural history of Iar-Connacht', 102–6.
52 Hardiman, *The history of the town and county of the town of Galway*.
53 Lamb, *Climate history*.
54 Fairley, *Irish beast book*.
55 E.H. Hogan, *The history of the Irish wolf-dog* (Dublin, 1897).
56 G.I. Dumville Lees, 'The last wolf killed in Ireland', *Land and Water*, 58 (1894), 611. See also Fairley, *Irish beast book*; Dumville Lees, 'The last wolf killed in Ireland', 689.
57 A. McFarland, *Hours in vacation: in five parts* (Dublin, 1853); N. Fisher McMillan, 'The wolf in Ireland', *Irish Naturalists' Journal*, 8:7 (1945), 261.
58 McFarland, *Hours in vacation*.
59 McCracken, *Irish woods*.
60 W. Harris (ed.), *The whole works of Sir James Ware concerning Ireland* (revised ed., Dublin, 1764).

61 Cabot, *Ireland*; Fairley, *Irish beast book*.
62 Allen, 'The wolf in Scotland and Ireland', 68–74; R. Fitter, *The Penguin dictionary of British natural history* (London, 1968); M. Burton (ed.), *The Shell natural history of Britain* (Norwich, 1970); McCracken, *Irish woods*; Foster, 'Encountering traditions', pp 23–70; Anon., 'Irish wolfdog supreme champion', *Carberry's Annual*, 1960/1 (Dublin, 1960); Harting, *British animals*; Richardson, 'Irish wolf-dog'.
63 Richardson, 'Irish wolf-dog'; J.E. Tennant, 'Wolves', *Notes and Queries*, 2:1 (1856), 282; Lydekker, *Royal natural history*; Lepus Hibernicus, 'The last wolf killed in Ireland', *Land and Water*, 58 (1894), 690; Allen, 'The wolf in Scotland and Ireland', 68–74.
64 J. Rutty, *An essay towards a natural history of the county of Dublin, accommodated to the noble designs of the Dublin Society*, 2 vols (Dublin, 1772).
65 R. Lewis, *The Dublin guide: or a description of the city of Dublin and the most remarkable places within fifteen miles* (Dublin, 1787).
66 Nuttall-Smith, *Chronicles of a Puritan family in Ireland*.
67 W.H. Workman, 'The wolf (*Canis lupus*) in Ireland', *Irish Naturalists' Journal*, 1:3 (1926), 43–4; Thompson, *Natural history of Ireland* iv; Allen, 'The wolf in Scotland and Ireland', 68–74.
68 P. O'Keeffe, pers. comm.
69 C.B. Moffat, *Life and letters of Alexander Goodman More* (Dublin, 1898)
70 Cabot, *Ireland: a natural history*; R. Lloyd Praeger, *Natural history of Ireland: a sketch of its flora and fauna* (London, 1950); Corballis, *Hunting in County Kilkenny*; G.A. Graham, 'Letter from G.A. Graham', *The Field*, 18 Sept. 1885; N. Fisher, 'The last Irish wolf', *Irish Naturalists' Journal*, 5:2 (1934), 41.
71 J. Edwards, 'Dances with wolves', *Sunday Tribune property supplement*, 8 Oct. 2000.
72 C.B. Moffat, 'The mammals of Ireland', *Proceedings of the Royal Irish Academy*, 44B (1938), 61–128.
73 Longfield, *Anglo-Irish trade*.
74 Flavin & Jones, *Bristol's trade with Ireland*.
75 Cahill, 'The wolf-men of Ossory', 12; P. O'Keeffe, pers. comm.; L.H. van Wijngaarden-Bakker, 'Littletonian faunas' in K.J Edwards & W. Warren (eds), *The quaternary history of Ireland* (London, 1985), pp 233–49.
76 N. Fisher McMillan, 'Last Irish wolves', *Irish Naturalists' Journal*, 17:3 (1971), 103.
77 Fairley, *Irish beast book*.
78 A. Kennedy, pers. comm.
79 C. Lewis, pers. comm.
80 Allen, 'The wolf in Scotland and Ireland', 68–74.
81 J. Ware, *De Hibernia et antiquitatibus eius or antiquities of Ireland* (London, 1658). See also Joyce, *A smaller social history*.
82 Thompson, *Natural history of Ireland*, iv.
83 Longfield, *Anglo-Irish trade*.
84 Ibid.
85 Anon., 'Irish wolfdog supreme champion'.
86 M. McBride, *The magnificent Irish wolfhound* (Dorking, 1998).
87 Kelly, *Early Irish farming*.
88 Longfield, *Anglo-Irish trade*.
89 Scharff, 'Wolf in Ireland', 133–6.
90 Harting, *British animals*.
91 Ibid.
92 E. Campion, *A historie of Ireland* (Dublin, 1633, facsimile ed. 1940).
93 C.A. Lewis, *Hunting in Ireland: an historical and geographical analysis* (London, 1975).
94 Harting, *British animals*.
95 J. Ware, *De Hibernia et antiquitatibus eius or antiquities of Ireland* (London, 1658).

96 Hogan, *The history of the Irish wolf-dog*.
97 Longfield, *Anglo-Irish trade*.
98 Allen, 'The wolf in Scotland and Ireland', 68–74.
99 J.P. O'Reilly, 'Notes on the history of the Irish wolf-dog', *Proceedings of the Royal Irish Academy*, 1 (1889–91), 333–9; Ball, 'Records of the export of Irish wolf-dogs', 101–2.
1 M. Colgan, 'An Irish naturalist in Spain in the eighteenth century', *Irish Naturalist*, 20 (1911), 1–5.
2 Ball, 'Records of the export of Irish wolf-dogs', 101–2.
3 G.A.Graham, *The Irish wolfhound* (Dursley, 1885).
4 Anon., 'Irish wolfdog supreme champion'; R. Lewis, *The Dublin guide: or a description of the city of Dublin and the most remarkable places within fifteen miles* (Dublin, 1787).
5 Ball, 'Records of the export of Irish wolf-dogs', 101–2.
6 R.P. Mahaffy (ed.), *Calendar of the state papers relating to Ireland preserved in the Public Record Office, 1666–1669* (London, 1908).
7 J. Graves, 'Transcript from a letter from W. Ellis secretary to the 1st duke of Ormonde to Captain George Mathews 11th March 1678/79', *Proceedings and Papers of the Kilkenny and South-East of Ireland Archaeological Society*, 2:1:1 (1856), 150.
8 Ball, 'Records of the export of Irish wolf-dogs', 101–2.
9 MacLysaght, *Irish life in the seventeenth century*, 4th ed.
10 Ibid.
11 Lewis, *Hunting in Ireland*.
12 Cox, *Gentleman's recreation*.
13 Thompson, *Natural history of Ireland*, iv; Anon., 'Irish wolfdog supreme champion'; E. Hull, *The physical geography and geology of Ireland* (London, 1878).
14 McCracken, *Irish woods*.

CHAPTER 6. POPULATION ESTIMATES AND WOLF ZOOLOGY FROM THE HISTORIC DATA

1 F. Kelly, *Early Irish farming: a study based mainly on the law-texts of the 7th and 8th centuries AD* (Dublin, 1997).
2 F.A. Allen, 'The wolf in Scotland and Ireland', *Transactions of the Caradoc and Severn Valley Field Club*, 5 (1909), 68–74.
3 P.W. Joyce, *A smaller social history of ancient Ireland* (London, 1908).
4 A.K. Longfield, *Anglo-Irish trade in the sixteenth century* (London, 1929).
5 Ibid.
6 Ibid.
7 S. Flavin & E.T. Jones (eds), *Bristol's trade with Ireland and the continent, 1503–1601: the evidence of the exchequer custom accounts* (Dublin, 2009).
8 Longfield, *Anglo-Irish trade*.
9 Ibid.; Flavin & Jones, *Bristol's trade*.
10 Longfield, *Anglo-Irish trade*; Flavin & Jones, *Bristol's trade*.
11 Longfield, *Anglo-Irish trade*.
12 Ibid.
13 Flavin & Jones, *Bristol's trade*.
14 Longfield, *Anglo-Irish trade*.
15 J.E. Harting, *British animals extinct within historic times* (London, 1880).
16 Ibid.
17 R.L. Grambo & D.J. Cox, *Wolf: legend, enemy, icon* (London, 2005).
18 E. McCracken, *The Irish woods since Tudor times: distribution and exploitation* (Belfast, 1971).

19 R. Dunlop, *Ireland under the Commonwealth* (Manchester, 1913).

20 D. Dickson, *New foundations Ireland, 1660–1800* (2nd ed., Dublin, 2000).

21 S. Pender (ed.), *A census of Ireland c.1659 with supplementary material from the Poll Money Ordinances (1660–1661)* (Dublin, 1939).

22 Federal Database on Wildlife, 'Biological data and habitat requirements', www.fs.fed.us/database/feis/animals, accessed 1 July 2011.

23 K.R. Hickey, 'A geographical perspective on the decline and extermination of the Irish Wolf *canis lupus*: an initial assessment', *Irish Geography*, 33:2 (2000), 185–98; K.R. Hickey, 'Where have all the wolves gone?' in J. Fenwick (ed.), *Lost and found II: discovering Ireland's past* (Wicklow, 2009), pp 29–40.

24 R.F. Scharff, 'The wolf in Ireland', *Irish Naturalist*, 31:12 (1922), 133–6.

25 Harting, *British animals*.

26 Dunlop, *Ireland under the Commonwealth*; J.P. Prendergast, *The Cromwellian settlement of Ireland* (3rd ed., Dublin, 1922).

27 D. Yalden & P. Barrett, *The history of British mammals* (London, 1999).

28 Dunlop, *Ireland under the Commonwealth*.

29 Prendergast, *Cromwellian settlement*; McCracken, *Irish woods*; E. MacLysaght, *Irish life in the seventeenth century* (4th ed., Dublin, 1979).

30 Ibid.

31 J. Fairley, *An Irish beast book: a natural history of Ireland's furred wildlife* (2nd ed., Belfast, 1984).

32 Barrett–Lennard, MS Papers (PRONI MS T.2529/6/104; Nov. 1696).

33 R.H. Busch, *The wolf almanac* (New York, revised ed., 1998).

34 Federal Database on Wildlife, 'Biological data and habitat requirements', www.fs.fed.us/database/feis/animals, accessed 1998.

35 S. Wavell, 'Tooth and claw', *Sunday Times travel supplement*, 8 Aug. 1999.

36 Grambo & Cox, *Wolf: legend, enemy, icon*.

37 Federal Database on Wildlife, 'Biological data and habitat requirements', www.fs.fed.us/database/feis/animals, accessed 1998.

38 N. Cox, *The gentleman's recreation, in four parts: viz. hunting, fowling, hawking, fishing, wherein those generous exercises are largely treated of* (1st ed., London, 1677), pp 106–9.

39 J. Waddell, *The prehistoric archaeology of Ireland* (Galway, 1998).

40 Cox, *Gentleman's recreation*.

41 R.F. Scharff, 'The Irish elk', *Irish Naturalist*, 1:6 (1926), 109–12.

42 T. Hammarstrom, *Nordic giant: the moose and its life* (Stockholm, 2004).

43 F. Mitchell & M. Ryan, *Reading the Irish landscape* (3rd ed., Dublin, 2001).

44 Cabot, *Ireland: a natural history*.

45 D. Hickie, *Native trees and forests of Ireland* (Dublin, 2002).

46 Kelly, *Early Irish farming*.

47 Fairley, *Irish beast book*.

48 Cox, *Gentleman's recreation*.

49 Wavell, 'Tooth and claw'.

50 Ethopian Wolf Conservation Project, www.ethopianwolf.org.

51 J. Brandenburg, 'Chasing summer', *BBC Wildlife Magazine* (July 2003).

52 A. Philps, 'Ravenous Thai workers devour Israeli wildlife', *Irish Independent*, 25 Apr. 2000.

53 Grambo & Cox, *Wolf: legend, enemy, icon*.

54 A. Cahill, 'The wolf-men of Ossory', *Ireland's Own*, 4,685 (1999), 12.

55 P. Ziegler, *The Black Death* (London, 1997).

56 P. O'Sullivan Beare, *Historiae Catholicae Iberniae compendium excusum a Petro Crasbeeckio, Ulyssippone* (Lisbon, 1621), ed. Matthew Kelly (Dublin, 1850); McCracken, *Irish woods*; C.A. Lewis, *Hunting in Ireland: an historical and geographical analysis* (London, 1975).

57 N. Hellen, 'Plan to bring wolves back to Scotland', *Sunday Times*, 24 Nov. 2004.

58 D. Yalden & P. Barrett, *The history of British mammals* (London, 1999).

59 J.D. O'Dowd, 'Stories about wolves', *Béaloideas*, 10 (1940), 287–9; Fairley, *Irish beast book*.

60 Hammarstrom, *Nordic giant*.

61 Fairley, *Irish beast book*.

62 Anon., 'Children attacked by wolves', *Sunday Tribune*, 17 Sept. 2003.

63 Grambo & Cox, *Wolf: legend, enemy, icon*.

64 www.scotsman.com, http://news.scotsman.com/latest.cfm?id=1742012005.

65 Indo-Asian News Service, www.newkerala.com/news-daily/news/features.php?action
    =fullnews&id=74035, accessed 2005.

CHAPTER 7. CAUSES OF THE DECLINE AND EXTERMINATION OF THE WOLF IN IRELAND

1   B. Schott, *Schott's food and drink miscellany* (London, 2003).

2   F. Kelly, *Early Irish farming: a study based mainly on the law-texts of the 7th and 8th centuries AD* (Dublin, 1997).

3   J.E. Harting, *British animals extinct within historic times* (London, 1880).

4   Cabot, *Ireland: a natural history*.

5   J.S. Brewer & W. Bullen, *Calendar of the Carew manuscripts preserved in the Archiepiscopal Library at Lambeth, 1575–1588* (London, 1868).

6   J. Fairley, *An Irish beast book: a natural history of Ireland's furred wildlife* (2nd ed., Belfast, 1984).

7   Brewer & Bullen, *Calendar of the Carew manuscripts*.

8   D. Cabot, *Ireland: a natural history* (London, 1999).

9   R.F. Scharff, 'The wolf in Ireland', *Irish Naturalist*, 31:12 (1922), 133–6.

10 Harting, *British animals*.

11 Cabot, *Ireland: a natural history*.

12 Fairley, *Irish beast book*.

13 Ibid.

14 T. Hammarstrom, *Nordic giant: the moose and its life* (Stockholm, 2004).

15 R.L. Grambo & D.J. Cox, *Wolf: legend, enemy, icon* (London, 2005).

16 Harting, *British animals*.

17 P. Steinhartt, *The company of wolves* (New York, 1995).

18 E. McCracken, *The Irish woods since Tudor times: distribution and exploitation* (Belfast, 1971).

19 Fairley, *Irish beast book*.

20 Harting, *British animals*.

21 J.W. Foster, 'Encountering traditions' in J.W. Foster & H.C.G. Chesney (eds), *Nature in Ireland: a scientific and cultural history* (Dublin, 1997), pp 23–70.

22 A. Cahill, 'The wolf-men of Ossory', *Ireland's Own*, 4,685 (1999), 12.

23 Ibid. From the Rushworths Collection. See also E. MacLysaght, *Irish life in the seventeenth century* (4th ed., Dublin, 1979).

24 McCracken, *Irish woods*.

25 R. Lloyd Praeger, *Natural history of Ireland: a sketch of its flora and fauna* (London, 1950).

26 C. Lewis, pers. comm.

27 J. Feehan, 'Threat and conservation: attitudes to nature in Ireland' in Foster & Chesney (eds), *Nature in Ireland*, pp 573–96.

28 J. Tierney, 'Woods and woodlands in early medieval Munster' in M.A. Monk & J. Sheehan (eds), *Early Medieval Munster: archaeology, history and society* (Cork, 1998), pp 53–64.

29 McCracken, *Irish woods*.

30 O. Rackman, *The history of the countryside* (London, 1986).

31 Tierney, 'Woods and woodlands in early medieval Munster', pp 53–64.
32 McCracken, *Irish woods*.
33 G. D'Arcy, *Ireland's lost birds* (Dublin, 1999).
34 E. Neeson, 'Woodland in history and culture' in Foster & Chesney (eds), *Nature in Ireland*, pp 133–56.
35 Foster, 'Encountering traditions'.
36 P. Sleeman, 'Mammals and mammology' in Foster & Chesney (eds), *Nature in Ireland*, pp 241–61.
37 Kelly, *Early Irish farming*.
38 MacLysaght, *Irish life in the seventeenth century*, 4th ed.
39 Cabot, *Ireland: a natural history*.
40 Foster, 'Encountering traditions', pp 23–70.
41 McCracken, *Irish woods*.
42 P. Gray, *The Irish Famine* (London, 1995).
43 Feehan, 'Threat and conservation', pp 573–96.
44 Ibid.
45 Foster, 'Encountering traditions'.
46 D.H. Chadwick, 'Wolf wars', *National Geographic*, 217:3 (2010), 34–55.

CHAPTER 8. FINAL COMMENTS

1 W.I. Montgomery, 'Phylogeography and conservation of the Irish hare', *Inaugural all Ireland mammal symposium: programme and abstracts* (2009), p. 27.
2 R.H. Busch, *The wolf almanac* (New York, rev. ed., 1998).
3 R.L. Grambo & D.J. Cox, *Wolf: legend, enemy, icon* (London, 2005).
4 Federal Database on Wildlife, 'Biological data and habitat requirements', www.fs.fed.us/database/feis/animals, accessed May 2011.
5 M. Viney, *A living island: Ireland's responsibility to nature* (Dublin, 2003).
6 G. D'Arcy, *Ireland's lost birds* (Dublin, 1999); The Golden Eagle Trust Ltd, www.goldeneagle.ie.
7 N. Hellen, 'Tycoon plans to return wolves to Highlands', *Sunday Times*, 12 Apr. 2003.
8 C. Haslam, 'Tipsy Thomas and the boys who cried wolf', *Sunday Times*, 25 May 2003.
9 S. Stafford, 'Wolves at our door: response', *BBC Wildlife Magazine*, 24:6 (2006), 93.
10 Grambo & Cox, *Wolf: legend, enemy, icon*.
11 J. McRae, 'Too many monarchs in the Glen', *BBC Wildlife Magazine* (June 2005), 29.
12 A.D. Manning, I.J. Gordon & W.J. Ripple, 'Restoring landscapes of fear with wolves in the Scottish Highlands', *Journal of Biological Conservation* (2009) (http://www.cof.orst.edu/leopold/papers/Manning%20et%20al%20%202009.pdf, accessed 8 June 2011).
13 S. Mills, 'Who'd be a wolf in Norway?', *BBC Wildlife Magazine* (Mar. 2005), 28–9.
14 I. Conway, 'Wolf hunt provokes urban outrage and rural satisfaction', *Irish Times*, 6 Jan. 2010.
15 Grambo & Cox, *Wolf: legend, enemy, icon*.
16 P. Robbins, J. Hintz & S.A. Moore, *Environment and society: a critical introduction* (London, 2010), pp 181–201.
17 J. Terborgh, 'Why we must bring back the wolf', *New York Review of Books*, 15 July 2010.
18 N. Hankins, 'Travel overseas: Abruzzo, Italy', *BBC Wildlife Magazine* (July 2005).
19 J. Cawley, 'Kings of the forest: on safari in wild Europe', *Sunday Times travel supplement*, 30 June 2002.
20 Anon., 'My, what big teeth you have', *Easyjet inflight magazine* (Mar. 2005).
21 Anon., *Hidden Valley Pet Farm promotional leaflet* (2005).
22 K. Davy, 'Wolves savage family pet', *Irish Star*, 12 Apr. 2001, pp 1, 4.

23 M. Rowlands, *The philosopher and the wolf: lessons from the wild on love, death and happiness* (London, 2008).
24 www.leerburg.com/wolf2.htm.
25 P.A. Cusdin & A.G. Greenwood, 'The keeping of wolf-hybrids in Great Britain', report prepared for the Department of the Environment, Transport and the Regions and the Royal Society for the Prevention of Cruelty to Animals, Research Contract CR0209 (2000).

Bibliography

RECOMMENDED READINGS ON WOLVES

Busch, R.H., *The wolf almanac* (revised ed., New York, 1998).
Grambo, R.L. & D.J. Cox, *Wolf: legend, enemy, icon* (London, 2005).
Mac Coitir, N., *Ireland's animals: myths, legends and folklore* (Cork, 2010).
Rowlands, M., *The philosopher and the wolf: lessons from the wild on love, death and happiness* (London, 2008).
Smith, J., *The wolf* (London, 2008).
Steinhart, P., *The company of wolves* (New York, 1995).

SOME USEFUL WEBSITES

Celtic names: www.daire.org.
Dublin Zoo: www.dublin.zoo.ie/come_arctic_wolves.htm.
Ethiopian Wolf Conservation Project: www.ethopianwolf.org.
Excavations: www.excavations.ie.
Golden Eagle Trust Ltd: www.goldeneagle.ie.
Griffith's Valuation: www.askaboutireland.ie/griffiths-valuation/index.
Irish place-names: www.logainm.ie.
Northern Ireland place-names: www.placenamesni.org.
USA Federal Database on Wildlife: www.fs.fed.us/database/feis/animals.
Woulfe surname: www.goireland.com/genealogy/family.htm?familyid=314.
    www.leerburg.com.

REFERENCES

Akinson, E.D., *An Ulster parish: being a history of Donaghcloney (Waringstown)* (Dublin, 1898).
Aldhouse Green, M., *Celtic Art: reading the messages* (London, 1996), 70, 94, 99, 127–37.
Allen, F.A., 'The wolf in Scotland and Ireland', *Transactions of the Caradoc and Severn Valley Field Club*, 5 (1909), 68–74.
Anon., *Co. Kildare in 1683*, TCD MS no. 1.1.2 (Dublin, 1683).

Anon., *The biography of a Tyrone family* (Belfast, 1829).

Anon., 'Illustrative notes to Sir Henry Sidney's memoir', *Ulster Journal of Archaeology*, 1:3 (1855), 43–52.

Anon., 'Irish wolfdog supreme champion', *Carberry's Annual* (1960/61), 9–11.

Anon., 'Parish of Breaffy', *School and parish: Breaffy, 1898–1990* (Sligo, 1990), p. 16.

Anon., 'Clare Island symposium, September 15–17, Clare Island, Co. Mayo', *Galway Advertiser*, 7 Sept. 2000.

Anon., 'Children attacked by wolves', *Sunday Tribune*, 17 Sept. 2003, 18.

Anon., 'My, what big teeth you have', *Easyjet inflight magazine*, Mar. 2005.

Anon., 'Hidden Valley Pet Farm' promotional leaflet (2005).

Archibald, C., & J. Bell, 'Wolves in Ireland', *Ulster Journal of Archaeology*, 2:1 (1854), 281.

Attenborough, D., *The life of mammals* (London, 2002), 131–5, 178–81, 300–2.

Attenborough, D., *Life in the undergrowth* (London, 2005), 133.

Automobile Association, *Book of the British countryside* (2nd ed., Basingstoke, 1974), 519.

Aybes, C., & D.W. Yalden, 'Place-name evidence for the former distribution of wolves and beavers in Britain', *Mammal Review*, 25:4 (2008), 201–26.

Ball, V., 'Records of the export of Irish wolf-dogs to the east in the 17th century', *Irish Naturalists' Journal*, 3:5 (1894), 101–2.

Barrett–Lennard, MS Papers, Public Records Office of Northern Ireland, MS T.2529/6/104, dated Nov. 1696.

Belozerskaya, M., *The Medici giraffe and other tales of exotic animals and power* (New York, 2006), 178–9.

Bennett, G., *History of Bandon* (Cork, 1869).

Blennerhassett, T., 'A direction for the Plantation of Ulster, containing in it six principal things', MS (1610).

Borrowes–Bart, E.D., 'The French settlers in Ireland, no. 6: the Huguenot colony at Portarlington, in the Queen's County continued', *Ulster Journal of Archaeology*, ser. 1, vol. 3 (1855), 213–9.

Bourke, A., S. Kilfeather, M. Luddy, M. Mac Curtain, G. Meaney, M. Ni Dhonnchadha, M. O'Dowd & C. Wills (eds), *The Field Day anthology of Irish writing*, IV and V: *Women's writing and traditions* (Cork, 2002).

Bourke, B., 'Rabbiting on, school and parish', *Breaffy 1898–1990* (Co. Sligo, 1990), 129.

Brandenburg, J., 'Chasing Summer', *BBC Wildlife* (July 2003), 52–3.

Brewer, J.S., & W. Bullen, *Calendar of the Carew manuscripts preserved in the Archiepiscopal Library at Lambeth, 1575–1588* (London, 1868), 401.

— *Calendar of the Carew manuscripts preserved in the Archiepiscopal Library at Lambeth, 1589–1600* (London, 1869), 245.

— *Calendar of the Carew manuscripts preserved in the Archiepiscopal Library at Lambeth* (London, 1873), 161–2

Briggs, M., & P. Briggs, *The natural history of the British Isles* (Bath, 2004), 202.

Broghill, Lord, 'Two letters from Lord Broghill to the Earl of Dorset', De La Warr MS, *Historic Manuscripts Commission Report*, no. 4 (1874), 280.

Brookes, R., *The art of angling, rock and sea-fishing: with the natural history of river, pond and sea-fish* (2nd ed., London, 1743).

Bryner, J., 'Africa's lone wolf: new species found in Ethopia', www.msnbc.msn. com/id/41315587/ns/technology_and_science-science/, accessed 2011.

Buczacki, S., *Fauna Britannica* (London, 2002), 11–2, 141–3, 316, 401–404, 419, 453.

Burke, W. P., *The Irish priest in the penal times (1660–1760): from the state papers and H.M. record office Dublin and London, the Bodleian Library and the British Museum* (Waterford, 1914, repr. 1969).

Burton, M. (ed.), *The Shell natural history of Britain* (Norwich, 1970), 461.

Busch, R.H., *The wolf almanac* (rev ed., New York, 1998).

Cabot, D., *Ireland: a natural history* (London, 1999), 16, 27, 68–70.

Cahill, A., 'The wolf-men of Ossory', *Ireland's Own*, 4:685 (1999), 12.

Cambrensis, G., *Topographia Hibernia, or, the history and topography of Ireland 1185*, trans. J.J. O'Meara (revised ed., Portlaoise, 1982), 24–5, 50–1, 70–2, 77, 115, 132–3.

Camden, W., *Britannia 1586* (1695 ed. Newton Abbot, facsimile ed. 1971).

Campion, E., *A historie of Ireland, 1570* (1633 ed. Dublin, facsimile ed. 1940).

Capella, P., 'Swiss afraid of the big, bad wolf', *The Guardian*, 2 Feb. 1999, 16.

Carey, N., 'Pro-acterial bee', *BBC Wildlife Magazine* (June 2005), 20.

Carruthers, T., *Kerry: a natural history* (Cork, 1998), 21, 124.

Carson, C., *The Táin: a new translation of the* Táin Bó Cúailnge (London, 2007), 92–4, 134, 203.

Caulfield, R., *The council book of the corporation of Youghal from 1690–1800* (1878).

Cawley, J., 'Kings of the forest: on safari in wild Europe', *Sunday Times travel supplement*, 30 June 2002, 3–4.

Chadwick, D.H., 'Wolf wars', *National Geographic*, 217:3 (2010), 34–55.

Coleman, J.C., & A.W. Stelfox, 'Excavation at Carrigtwohill Caves, Co. Cork', *Irish Naturalists' Journal*, 8:8 (1945), 299–302.

Colgan, M., 'An Irish naturalist in Spain in the eighteenth century', *Irish Naturalists' Journal*, 20 (1911), 1–5.

Compton, J., *A compendious system of chronology* (Belfast, 1823).

Connolly, S., & A. Moroney, *Ogham ancestors remembered in stone* (Drogheda, 2000), 27.

Conway, I., 'Wolf hunt provokes urban outrage and rural satisfaction', *Irish Times*, 6 May 2010.

Coombs, D., *Sport and the countryside in the English paintings, watercolours and prints* (New York, 1978).

Corballis, C., *Hunting in County Kilkenny* (Gowran, Co. Kilkenny, 1999), 26.

Corbet G.B., & S. Harris (eds), *The handbook of British mammals* (Oxford, 1991).

Cosimo III *Travels of Cosimo the third, Grand Duke of Tuscany, through England during the reign of King Charles the second 1669. Translated from the Italian MS in the Laurentian library at Florence. To which is prefixed, a memoir of his life* (London, 1821).

Cox, N., *The gentleman's recreation, in four parts. viz. hunting, fowling, hawking, fishing. Wherein those generous exercises are largely treated of* (London, 1677).

Croaffts, C., 'Wolves, two letters from Christopher Croaffts to Sir John Perceval', Egmont manuscripts, *Historic Manuscripts Commission Report*, 2 (1909), 5.

Crossly, A., *The significance of most things that are born in heraldry with the explanation of their natural qualities* (Dublin, 1724).

Cunningham, G., & R. Coghlan, *The mystery animals of Ireland* (Bideford, North Devon, 2010), 53, 86, 93–6, 133, 140, 147–52.

Ormond, *Calendar of Ormond deeds, 1172–1350* [etc.], ed. E. Curtis (Dublin, 1932).

Cusdin, P.A., & A.G. Greenwood, *The keeping of wolf-hybrids in Great Britain*, report prepared for the UK Department of the Environment, Transport and the Regions and the Royal Society for the Prevention of Cruelty to Animals, Research Contract CR0209 (2000).

D'Alton, E.A., *History of Ireland: from the earliest times to the present day*, half vol. 4, *1649 to 1782* (London, 1920), 356–7.

D'Arcy, G., *Ireland's lost birds* (Dublin, 1999), 25, 34–5.

Davison, A.H., J. Orr, A.W. Stelfox & J.A.S. Stendall, 'Excavations of White Park Bay kitchen midden site', *Irish Naturalists' Journal*, 1:14 (1927), 280–2, 284.

Davy, K., 'Wolves savage family pet', *Irish Star*, 12 Apr. 2001, 1 & 4.

De Bhulb, S., *Sloinnte Uile Eireann: all Ireland surnames, Comhar-Chumann Ide Naofa* (2002).

Derrick, J., 'Image of Ireland', *Lord Somer's tracts*, 1 (1581), 579.

Di Martino, V., *Roman Ireland* (Cork, 2003), 125–6.

Dickson, D., *New foundations Ireland, 1660–1800* (2nd ed. Dublin, 2000).

Dillon, P., *Connemara: Collins rambler guide* (London, 2001), 110.

Doherty, J.E., & D.J. Hickey, *A chronology of Irish history since 1500* (Dublin, 1989), 53.

Dowd, M., 'Glencurran Cave, Tullycommon, Co. Clare' online at www.excavations.ie/Pages/Details.php?Year =&County=Clare&id=11108, accessed 1 July 2011.

Duffy, P., *Landscapes of South Ulster: a parish atlas of the Diocese of Clogher* (Belfast, 1993), 109, 112.

Dumville Lees, G.I., 'The last wolf killed in Ireland', *Land and Water*, 58 (1894), 611.

— 'The last wolf in Ireland', *Land and Water*, 58 (1894), 689.

Dunlop, R., *Ireland under the Commonwealth* (Manchester, 1913).

Dunne, J., 'Folklore no.1: the Fenian traditions of Sliabh-Na-M-Ban', *Transactions of the Kilkenny Archaeological Society*, 1:3 (1851), 333–62.

Echard, L., *An exact description of Ireland* (London, 1691).

Edwards, A., *Edward's Cork remembrancer; or, tablet of memory. Enumerating every remembrance circumstance that has happenned in the city and county of Cork and in the kingdom at large. Including all the memorable events in Great Britain ... also the remarkable earthquakes, famines ... fires, and all other accidents of moment in every quarter of the globe, from the earliest period, to the 1792* (Cork, 1792).

Edwards, J., 'Dances with wolves', *Sunday Tribune property supplement*, 8 Oct. 2000, 2.

Edwards, K.J. & W. Warren (eds), *The quaternary history of Ireland* (London, 1985), pp 233–49.

Eliot, C.W., *Epic and Saga* (Montana, 2003).

Fairley, J., *Irish wild mammals: a guide to the literature* (Galway, 1972).

— 'Exports of wild mammal skins from Ireland in the eighteenth century', *Irish Naturalists' Journal*, 21:2 (1983), 75–9.

— *An Irish beast book: a natural history of Ireland's furred wildlife* (2nd ed., Belfast, 1984).

— *Irish wild mammals: a guide to the literature* (2nd ed., Galway, 1992).

— *A basket of weasels: the weasel family in Ireland and other furred Irish beasts: bats, the rabbit, hares and some rodents* (Belfast, 2001), 135, 268.

Falls, C., *Elizabeth's Irish wars* (repr. ed., London, 1996), 220, 224, 248, 335.

Feehan, J., 'The heritage of the rocks', in J.W. Foster, & H.C.G. Chesney (eds), *Nature in Ireland: a scientific and cultural history* (Dublin, 1997), pp 3–22.

— 'Threat and conservation: attitudes to nature in Ireland' in J.W. Foster & H.C.G. Chesney (eds), *Nature in Ireland: a scientific and cultural history* (Dublin, 1997), pp 573–96.

Fisher McMillan, N., 'The wolf in Ireland', *Irish Naturalists' Journal*, 8:7 (1945), 261.

— 'Last Irish wolves', *Irish Naturalists' Journal*, 17:3 (1971), 103.

— 'The last Irish wolf', *Irish Naturalists' Journal*, 5:2 (1934), 41.

Fitter, R., *The Penguin dictionary of British natural history* (London, 1968), 285.

FitzPatrick, E., M. O'Brien, & P. Walsh (eds), *Archaeological investigations in Galway City, 1987–1998* (Wicklow, 2004).

Flanagan, D., & L. Flanagan, *Irish place names* (Dublin, 1994).

Flanagan, L., 'An index to minor place-names from the 6-inch Ordnance Survey: Co. Derry', *Bulletin of the Ulster place-name society*, ser. 2, vol. 2 (1979), 61–74.

— 'An Index to Minor Place-Names from the 6-inch Ordnance Survey: Co. Armagh', *Bulletin of the Ulster place-name society*, ser. 2, vol. 4 (1981–2), 76–84.

Flannery, T., & P. Schouten, *A gap in nature: discovering the world's extinct animals* (London, 2001).

Flavin, S., & E.T. Jones (eds), *Bristol's trade with Ireland and the Continent 1503–1601: the evidence of the exchequer custom accounts* (Dublin, 2009).

Forrest, H.E., 'Prehistoric mammals of Ireland: II', *Irish Naturalists' Journal*, 1:8 (1926), 152–3.
— 'Prehistoric mammals of Ireland: IV continued', *Irish Naturalists' Journal*, 1:12 (1927), 234–6.
Foster, J.W., 'Encountering traditions' in J.W. Foster & H.C.G. Chesney (eds), *Nature in Ireland: a scientific and cultural history* (1997a), pp 23–70.
— 'Nature and nation in the nineteenth century', in J.W. Foster & H.C.G. Chesney (eds), *Nature in Ireland: a scientific and cultural history* (1997), pp 409–39.
Great Britain Census Office (GBCO), *Census of Ireland, 1851: supplementary report on tables of death* (London, 1852), 103–6.
Graham, G.A., 'Letter from G.A. Graham', *The Field*, 18 Sept. 1885.
— *The Irish wolfhound* (Dursley, 1885), 1–47.
Grambo, R.L., & D.J. Cox, *Wolf: legend, enemy, icon* (London, 2005).
Graves, J., 'Transcript from a letter from W. Ellis, secretary to the 1st Duke of Ormonde, to Captain George Mathews, 11 Mar. 1678–9', *Proceedings and papers of the Kilkenny and South-East of Ireland Archaeological Society*, ser. 2, 1:1 (1856), 150.
Gray, P., *The Irish Famine* (London, 1995).
Green, D., & F. O'Connor (eds), *A golden treasury of Irish poetry AD 600 to 1200* (London, 1967).
Grub, J., 'The wolf-days of Ireland', *Zoologist*, 20 (1862), 7996–7.
Hammarstrom, T., *Nordic giant: the moose and its life* (Stockholm, 2004), 35–6, 74, 80, 86, 92–3.
Hankins, N., 'Travel overseas: Abruzzo, Italy', *BBC Wildlife Magazine* (July 2005).
Hanson, N., *The confident hope of a miracle: the story of the Spanish Armada* (London, 2005).
Hardiman, J., *The history of the town and county of the town of Galway* (Dublin, 1820).
Harris, W., (ed.), *The whole works of Sir James Ware concerning Ireland* (revised ed., Dublin, 1764).
Harting, J.E., *British animals extinct within historic times* (London, 1880).
Haslam, C., 'Tipsy Thomas and the boys who cried wolf', *Sunday Times*, 25 May 2003, 14.
Heaney, Seamus, *Wintering Out* (London: 1972).
Hellen, N., 'Tycoon plans to return wolves to Highlands', *Sunday Times*, 12 Apr. 2003, 23
— 'Plan to bring wolves back to Scotland', *Sunday Times*, 22 Nov. 2004, 4.
Hepworth Holland, C., *The Irish landscape: a scenery to celebrate* (Edinburgh, 2003).
Her Majesty's Stationery Office (HMSO) *Census of Ireland: general alphabetical index to the townlands and towns, parishes and baronies of Ireland* (Dublin, 1861).
Herbert, T., 'Wolves in Ireland', *Zoologist*, 3:9 (1885), 268.

Hickey, K.R., 'A geographical perspective on the decline and extermination of the Irish Wolf, *canis lupus*: an initial assessment', *Irish Geography*, 33:2 (2000), 185–98.

— 'Wolf: forgotten Irish hunter', *Wild Ireland*, 3 (2003), 10–13.

— 'The history of wolves in Ireland', *Wolfprint*, 24 (2005), 10–13.

— 'Where have all the wolves gone?' in J. Fenwick (ed.), *Lost and found II: discovering Ireland's past* (Wicklow, 2009), pp 29–40.

Hickie, D., *Native trees and forests of Ireland* (Dublin, 2002), 4, 107.

Higgins, M.J., 'Wolves and foxes in Irish folklore' (BA, NUIG, 2007).

Hogan, E.H., *The history of the Irish wolf-dog* (Dublin, 1897), 164–71.

Hole, C., (ed.), *The encyclopedia of superstitions* (Oxford, 1980), 154–7, 166, 275.

Hooker, J., (ed.), *Holinshed's chronicles of England, Scotland and Ireland* (2nd ed., London, 1586).

Hull, E., *The physical geography and geology of Ireland* (London, 1878), 270–2.

Jackson, K.H., *A Celtic miscellany: translations from the Celtic literature* (London, 1951).

Jones, M., 'The man from South Yorkshire who had the privilege of seeing one of the last surviving wolves in the British Isles', *Sorby Record*, 36 (2000), 28–31.

Joyce, P.W., *The origin and history of Irish names of places*, 3 vols (Dublin, 1891; facsimile repr. 1995), vol. I 480–2, vol. III 149.

— *A smaller social history of ancient Ireland* (London, 1908).

K'eogh, J., *Zoologia Medicinalis Hibernica* (Dublin, 1739), 91–7.

Keck, P.E., H.G. Pope, J.L. Hudson, S.L. McElroy & A.R. Kulick, 'Lycanthropy: alive and well in the twentieth century', *Psychological Medicine*, 18:1 (1988), 113–120.

Kelly, F., *Early Irish farming: a study based mainly on the law-texts of the 7th and 8th centuries AD*, Early Irish Law, 9 (Dublin, 1997), 38–9, 49, 114, 119, 130, 178, 186–9, 282, 352.

Kenny, C., *Molaise: Abbot of Leighlin and hermit of Holy Island, Killala* (Co. Mayo, 1998), 84.

Koehler, C., & P. Richardson, '*Proteles cristatus*', *Mammalian Species*, 363 (1990), 1–6.

Lacey, J., *A candle in the window* (Dublin, 1999).

Lamb, H.H., *Climate history and the modern world* (2nd ed., London, 1985), 206, 224, 244, 315.

Lang, J.T., 'Viking Age decorated wood: a study of its ornament and style', *Medieval Dublin excavations, 1962–1981*, ser. B, vol. 1 (1988).

Lecky, W.E.H., *A history of Ireland in the 18th century*, 1 (new ed., London, 1892).

Leith Adams, A., 'Report on the exploration of Shandon Cave', *Transactions of the Royal Irish Academy*, 26 (1876), 187–230.

— 'Explorations in the Bone Cave of Ballinamintra', *Transactions of the Royal Dublin Society*, 7:2 (1881), 177–266.

Lepus Hibernicus, 'The last wolf killed in Ireland', *Land and Water*, 58 (1894), 690.

— *Hunting in Ireland: an historical and geographical analysis* (London, 1975), 37–43.

Lewis, R., *The Dublin guide: or a description of the city of Dublin and the most remarkable places within fifteen miles* (Dublin, 1787).

Lloyd Praeger, R., 'Botanizing in the Ards', *Irish Naturalists' Journal*, 12:2 (1903), 254–65.

— *Natural history of Ireland: a sketch of its flora and fauna* (London, 1950), 13, 83–5, 180–1, 196–7.

— *The way that I went: an Irishman in Ireland* (Cork, 1997), 140, 242, 328–9.

Longfield, A.K., *Anglo-Irish trade in the sixteenth century* (London, 1929), 64, 69–71, 94–7, 214.

Lowe, E.J., *Natural phenomena and chronology of the seasons; being an account of remarkable frosts, droughts, thunderstorms, gales, floods, earthquakes, etc, also diseases, cattle plagues, famines etc, which have occurred in the British Isles since A.D. 220, chronologically arranged* (London, 1870), 15.

Lunham, T.A., 'Bishop Dive Downes' visitation of his Diocese, 1699–1702', *Journal of the Cork Historical and Archaeological Society*, 15 (1909), 163–80.

Lydekker, R., (ed.), *The royal natural history*, 1 (London, 1894), 497.

Lyng, T., *Castlecomer Connections* (Co. Kilkenny, 1984).

Lysaght, S., 'Contrasting natures: the issue of names' in J.W. Foster & H.C.G. Chesney (eds), *Nature in Ireland: a scientific and cultural history* (1997), pp 440–60.

Mac Coitir, N., *Ireland's animals: myths, legends and folklore* (Cork, 2010).

Macauley, T.B., *History of England from the accession of James I*, 5 vols (Philadelphia, 1848).

Mackenzie, C., *The natural history of all the most remarkable quadrupeds, birds, fishes, reptiles and insects; abridged from Buffon, Goldsmith, Cuvier, and other eminent naturalists. With upwards of one hundred beautiful cuts* (London, 1860).

MacLysaght, E., *Irish life in the seventeenth century* (2nd ed., Cork, 1950).

— *Irish life in the seventeenth century* (4th ed., Dublin, 1979), 4, 108–9, 137–43.

Maguire, S.J., 'Some notes on the natural history of Iar-Connacht in the seventeenth century', *Galway Reader*, 4:2/3 (1954), 102–6.

Mahaffy, R.P. (ed.), *Calendar of the state papers relating to Ireland preserved in the Public Record Office, 1647–1660* (London, 1903), 641.

— *Calendar of the state papers relating to Ireland preserved in the Public Record Office, 1663–1665* (London, 1907), 637–8, 649.

— *Calendar of the state papers relating to Ireland preserved in the Public Record Office, 1666–1669* (London, 1908), 408–483.

Manning, A.D., L.J. Gordon, & W.J. Ripple, 'Restoring landscapes of fear with wolves in the Scottish Highlands', *Journal of Biological Conservation* (2009), online at doi:10.1016/j.biocon.2009.05.007, accessed 8 April 2011.

Marnell, F., N. Kingston, & D. Looney, *Ireland red list no. 3: terrestrial mammals* (Dublin, 2009).

Matheson, R.E, *Special report on surnames in Ireland, 1890* (Dublin, 1894).

Matthews, J., *Celtic totem animals* (Boston, 2002).

McBride, M., *The magnificent Irish wolfhound* (Dorking, 1998).

McCormick, F., 'Early evidence for wild animals in Ireland' in N. Benecke (ed.), *The Holocene history of the European vertebrate fauna*, Archaologie Eurasien Band 6 (1999), 355–71.

McCracken, E., *The Irish woods since Tudor times: distribution and exploitation* (Belfast, 1971), 14, 20, 28–30, 46–7.

McFarland, A., *Hours in vacation: in five parts* (Dublin, 1853).

McManus, D., *A guide to Ogam*, Maynooth monographs, no. 4 (1991), 102, 105–7, 113, 177.

McNeill C., 'Down Survey map of Ballybay, Co. Offaly (1655–1656), copies of Down Survey maps in private collections', *Analecta Hibernica*, 8 (1938), 419–28.

McRae, J., 'Too many monarchs in the glen', *BBC Wildlife Magazine* (June 2005), 29.

McWilliams, B., *Weather Eye: the final year* (Dublin, 2009), 80–1.

Meyer, K., *Contributions to Irish lexicography*, i: *A-C* (London, 1906).

Miege, G., *The present state of Great Britain and Ireland in three parts ... containing an accurate and impartial account of these great and famous islands, of their several counties and their inhabitants ... of the vast, populous and opulent city of London ... of the Britains original, language, temper, genius, religion, morals, trade ... with the lists of the present officers in church and state ... to which are added, maps of the three kingdoms, also the present state of His Majesty's dominions in Germany ... and a new map of them all* (London, 1707).

Mills, S., 'Who'd be a wolf in Norway?', *BBC Wildlife Magazine* (Mar. 2005), 28–9.

Mitchell, F., & M. Ryan, *Reading the Irish landscape* (3rd ed., Dublin, 2001), 91–2, 236.

Moffat, C.B., *Life and letters of Alexander Goodman More* (Dublin, 1898).

— 'The mammals of Ireland', *Proceedings of the Royal Irish Academy*, 44B (1938), 61–128.

Montgomery, W.I., 'Phylogeography and conservation of the Irish hare', *Inaugural All Ireland mammal symposium: programme and abstracts* (2009), 27.

Moore, D., *The accidental pilgrim: travels with a Celtic saint* (Dublin, 2004)

Moriarty, C., 'The early naturalists' in J.W. Foster & H.CG. Chesney, *Nature in Ireland: a scientific and cultural history* (1997), 71–90.

Moryson, Fynes *An itinerary: containing his ten years travel through the twelve dominions of Germany, Bohemia, Switzerland, Netherland, Denmark, Poland, Italy, Turkey, France, England, Scotland and Ireland 1617*, 3 vols (London, 1735), ii, (*History of Ireland, 1599–1603, with a short narrative of the state of the kingdom from 1169*).

Murphy, P., *Cuchulain's leap: a history of the parishes of Carrigaholt and Cross* (Carrigaholt and Cross, 1992).

Neeson, E., 'Woodland in history and culture' in Foster & Chesney (eds), *Nature in Ireland* (1997), pp 133–56.

Newman, C., 'Ballinderry crannóg no. 2, Co. Offaly: pre-crannóg early medieval horizon', *The Journal of Irish Archaeology*, 11 (2002), 99–123.

Nolan, P., 'The wolves of Co. Clare', *The Other Clare*, 28 (2004), 63–8.

Nuttall-Smith, G.N., *The chronicles of a Puritan family in Ireland* (Oxford, 1923).

Ó Hógáin, D., *Irish superstitions* (Dublin, 1995), 34.

Ó Riain, F., 'Where's that: Bunratty, 1425', *Irish Times*, 2 Dec. 2002, 3.

— 'Where's that: Ballymorgan, 1453', *Irish Times*, 20 June 2003, 3.

Ó Súilleabháin, S., *A handbook of Irish folklore* (Detroit, 1970), 297.

O'Boyle, S., *Ogam: the poets' secret* (Dublin, 1980), 15.

O'Callaghan, S., *To Hell or Barbados: the ethnic cleansing of Ireland* (Dingle, 2000), 55.

O'Daly, M., (ed.), *The heroic biography of Cormac mac Airt, Cath Maige Mucrama: the battle of Mag Mucrama* (Dublin, 1975).

O'Donovan, J., *Ordnance Survey letters, Londonderry: letters relating to the antiquities of County Londonderry containing information collected during progress of the Ordnance Survey in 1837* (Dublin, 1834).

— *Ordnance Survey letters, Wicklow: letters relating to the antiquities of County Wicklow containing information collected during progress of the Ordnance Survey in 1838* (Dublin, 1838).

— (ed.), *Annala Rioghachta Eireann, Annals of the Kingdom of Ireland, by the Four Masters, from the earliest period to the year 1616*, 6 vols (Dublin, 1851).

O'Dowd, J.D., 'Stories about wolves', *Béaloideas*, 10 (1940), 287–9.

O'Dowd, M., *Calendar of state papers, Ireland, Tudor Period, 1571–1575* (Kew, 2000), 279.

O'Flaherty, R., *A chorographical description of west or H-Iar Connaught, edited with notes an illustrations by J. Hardiman* (1684; Dublin, 1846).

O'Reilly, J.P., 'Notes on the history of the Irish wolf-dog', *Proceedings of the Royal Irish Academy*, 1 (1889–91), 333–9.

— 'On the waste of the coast of Ireland as a factor in Irish history', *Proceedings of the Royal Irish Academy, section B – biological, geological and chemical science*, 24:2 (1902), 95–202.

O'Sullivan, S., (ed.), *Folktales of Ireland* (London, 1966), 27–9.

O'Sullivan Beare, P., *Historiae Catholicae Iberniae Compendium excusum a Petro Crasbeeckio, Ulyssippone* (Lisbon, 1621), ed. M. Kelly (Dublin, 1850).

Pender, S., (ed.), *A census of Ireland c.1659 with supplementary material from the Poll Money Ordinances (1660–1661)* (Dublin, 1939).

Philps, A., 'Ravenous Thai workers devour Israeli wildlife', *Irish Independent*, 25 Apr. 2000, 16.

Pickering, D., *Dictionary of superstitions* (London, 1998), 285, 290.

Plummer, C., *Vitae sanctorum Hibernia*, 1 (Oxford, 1910).

Powers, J., 'Wonderful wolf peach', *Irish Times Saturday Magazine*, 17 May 2004, 22–23.

Prendergast, J.P., *The Cromwellian settlement of Ireland* (3rd ed., Dublin, 1922), 308–11.

Prim, J.G.A., 'Petition from William Collowe to the Duke of Ormond dated 29 Apr. 1663, for permission to kill wolves', *The Journal of the Kilkenny and South-East of Ireland Archaeological Society*, ser. 6 (1867), 211–12.

Quinn, D.B., 'The Munster plantation: problems and opportunities', *Journal of the Cork Historical and Archaeological Society*, 71 (1966), 19–40.

Quinn, H., 'Dramatic seascape frames rugged Wolf Hill', *Sunday Tribune Business Supplement*, 20 Nov. 2005, 3.

Rackman, O., *The history of the countryside* (London, 1986).

Raftery, B., *Pagan Celtic Ireland: the enigma of the Irish Iron Age* (New York, 1994), 17, 126.

Rhys, J., 'The Ogham inscribed stones in the collection of the Royal Irish Academy', *The Journal of the Royal Society of Antiquaries of Ireland*, 32 (1902), 1–43.

Richardson, H.D., 'The Irish wolf-dog', *Irish Penny Journal* (1841).

Robbins, P., J. Hintz, & S.A. Moore, *Environment and society: a critical introduction.* (London, 2010), pp 181–201.

Rowlands, M., *The philosopher and the wolf: lessons from the wild on love, death and happiness* (London, 2008).

Russell, C.W., & J.P. Prendergast, *Calendar of the state papers relating to Ireland preserved in the Public Record Office and elsewhere, 1611–1614* (London, 1877), 192.

Rutty, J., *An essay towards a natural history of the county of Dublin, accommodated to the noble designs of the Dublin Society*, 2 vols (Dublin, 1772).

Savile, H., & A. Marwell, *Advice to a painter: being a satyr upon the French King, Admiral Tourvill, Irish camp at Havre de Grace, murmuring, Jacobites &c, printed for Randall Taylor* (1692).

Scharff, R.F., 'The wolf in Ireland', *Irish Naturalists' Journal*, 31:12 (1922), 133–6.

— 'The wolf in Ireland', *Irish Naturalists' Journal*, 33 (1924), 95.

— 'The Irish Elk', *Irish Naturalists' Journal*, 1:6 (1926), 109–12.

— H.J. Seymour & E.T. Newton, 'Exploration of Castlepook Cave, Co. Cork', *Proceedings of the Royal Irish Academy*, 34B (1918), 33–72.

— R.J. Ussher, G.A.J. Cole, E.T. Newton, A.F. Dixon & T.J. Westropp, 'The exploration of the caves of Co. Clare: being the second report from the Committee appointed to explore Irish caves', *Transactions of Royal Irish Academy*, 33B:1 (1906), 1–76.

Scheinfeld, N.S., & V. Deleo, 'Photosensitivity in lupus erythematosus', *Photodermatology Photoimmunology Photomedecine*, 20 (2004), 272–9.

Schott, B., *Schott's food and drink miscellany* (London, 2003), 85.

Simons, P., *Weird Weather* (London, 1996), 224.

Sinclair, J., *Statistical account of Scotland*, xii: *north and west Perthshire* (Edinburgh, 1791–9).

Sleeman, P., 'Mammals and Mammology' in Foster & Chesney (eds), *Nature in Ireland* (1997), pp 241–61.

Smith, C., *Ancient and present state of the county of Kerry* (Dublin, 1756).

Smith, J., *The wolf* (London, 2008).

Smith, J., 'Climate change linked to floods and heatwaves', *Irish Times*, 29 Nov. 2005, p. 10.

Speede, J., *The theatre of the empire of Great Britaine* (London, 1612).

Stafford, S., 'Wolves at our door: response', *BBC Wildlife Magazine*, 24:6 (2006), 93.

Steinhart, P., *The company of wolves* (New York, 1995).

Stout, M., *The Irish ringfort* (Dublin, 1997).

Stuart, A.J., & L.H. van Wijngaarden-Bakker, 'Quaternary Vertebrates' in Edwards & Warren (eds), *The quaternary history of Ireland* (1985), pp 221–33.

Swift, C., *Ogam stones and the earliest Irish Christians* (Maynooth, 1997), 70.

Tennant, J.E, 'Wolves', *Notes and Queries*, ser. 2, vol. 1 (1856), 282.

Terborgh, J., 'Why we must bring back the wolf', *New York Review of Books*, 15 July 2010.

Thomas, E.A., *Fish, flesh and good red herring* (London, 2004), 203.

Thomas, K., *Man and the natural world: changing attitudes in England, 1500–1800* (London, 1984).

Thompson, W., *Belfast and its environs with a tour to the Giant's Causeway: containing a map, plan, and numerous illustrations on wood* (Dublin, 1842).

— *Natural history of Ireland*, iv: *Mammalia, reptiles and fishes also invertebrata* (London, 1856), 33–5.

Tierney, J., 'Woods and woodlands in early medieval Munster' in M.A. Monk & J. Sheehan (eds), *Early Medieval Munster: archaeology, history and society* (Cork, 1998), pp 53–64.

Todd, J.H., (ed.), *The Irish version of the Historia Britonum of Nennius* (Dublin, 1848).

Trimmer, S., *A description of a set of prints of English history; contained in a set of easy lessons* (London, 1792).

Tuberville, G., *The noble art of venerie or hunting, wherein is handled and set out, the vertues, natures, and properties of fifteene sundrie chaces, together with the order and maner how to hunte and kill everyone of them. Translated and collected, for pleasure of all noblemen and gentlemen, out of the best approved authors which have written anything concerning the same, and reduced into such order and proper termes as are used here in the noble eealme of Englande* (London, 1575).

Tynan, T., 'Ancient Christian burial at Wolfhill, Kilfeacle, Co. Leix', *Journal of the Royal Society of Antiquaries of Ireland*, con. ser. 62 (1932), 119–20.

van Wijngaarden-Bakker, L.H., 'Littletonian faunas' in Edwards & Warren (eds) *The quaternary history of Ireland* (1985), pp 233–49.

— 'Faunal remains and the Irish Mesolithic' in C. Bonesll (ed.), *The Mesolithic in Europe* (Edinburgh, 1989), pp 125–33.

Viney, M., 'Wild sports and stone guns' in J.W. Foster & H.C.G. Chesney (eds), *Nature in Ireland: a scientific and cultural history* (1997), pp 524–48.

— *Ireland: a Smithsonian natural history* (Belfast, 2003).

— *A living island: Ireland's responsibility to nature* (Dublin, 2003).

Waddell, J., 'Rathcroghan: a royal site in Connacht', *The Journal of Irish Archaeology*, 1 (1983), 21–46.
— *The prehistoric archaeology of Ireland* (Galway, 1998), 1, 10–4, 19, 22.
Ware, J., *De Hibernia et Antiquitatibus eius, or, Antiquities of Ireland* (London, 1658).
Wavell, S., 'Tooth and claw', *Sunday Times Travel Supplement*, 8 Aug. 1999, 1–2.
Webber, C.T., 'Untitled note', *Proceedings of the Royal Irish Academy*, 2 (1841).
Wendelin, D., D. Pope, & S. Mallory, 'Hypertrichosis', *Journal of the American Academy of Dermatology*, 48:2 (2003), 161–79.
Westropp, T.J., *Folklore of Clare: a folklore survey of County Clare and County Clare folk tales and myths* (Ennis, 2000).
Whilde, T., *The natural history of Connemara* (London, 1994), 49.
Whitfield, P., (ed.), *The Marshall illustrated encyclopedia of animals* (London, 1998), 180–181.
Wilde, Lady, *Irish cures, mystic charms and superstitions* (New York, 1991).
Williams, S., 'Wolves on high', *BBC Wildlife Magazine* (July 2004), 30–5.
Windisch, E., *Irische Text mit Übersetzungen und Wörterbuch*, 1 (Berlin, 1880).
Woodman, P., M. McCarthy & N. Monaghan, 'The Irish quaternary fauna project', *Quaternary Science Reviews*, 2 (1997), 129–59.
Wood-Martin, W.G., *History of Sligo: county and town from the close of the revolution of 1688 to the present time* (Dublin, 1892), 273.
Workman, W.H., 'The wolf (*Canis lupus*) in Ireland', *Irish Naturalists' Journal*, 1:3 (1926), 43–4.
World Conservation Monitoring Centre, *Endangered Mammals!* (Chicago, 1995).
Yalden, D., P. Barrett, *The history of British mammals* (London, 1999).
Young, R.M., 'Query concerning the source from which J. Compton derived the information given in *A compendious system of chronology* that the last wolf seen in Ireland was killed at Aughnabrack, near Belfast', *Ulster Journal of Archaeology*, ser. 2, vol. 2 (1896), 143.
Young, S., *A.D. 500: a journey through the dark isles of Britain and Ireland* (London, 2005), 29, 33, 53, 166–7.
Ziegler, P., *The Black Death* (London, 1997), 67, 90.
Zuppiroli, P., & L. Donnez, 'The Mexican wolf', *Wolf Print*, 22 (2005), 16–19.

Index